THE PRINCE, THE PRIESTS & THE PROPHETS

The Need for Prophetic Leadership in America

Lisa,
I hope this is an enjoyable read. More importantly, I hope you are prospering and enduring!

Kyle J. Boyer

RX2
PUBLISHING

THE PRINCE, THE PRIESTS & THE PROPHETS by Kyle J. Boyer
RX2 Publishing
Coatesville, PA 19320

Unless otherwise noted, all scripture quotations are from the New Revised Standard Version of the Bible. Copyright © 1989 by the Division of Christian Education of the National Council of the Churches of Christ in the United States of America. All rights reserved.

Scripture quotations marked KJV are from the King James Version of the Bible. Public domain.

ISBN-13: 978-0-9998175-1-3 (paperback)

To every man or woman who has sacrificed for the cause of prophetic witness.

Contents

Introduction
THREE OFFICES

For years, *Time* magazine covers have expressed the issues that have dominated America's consciousness at a given moment. Although I've never been a regular patron of the magazine, I have often taken note of what's on the cover. The cover of the May 11, 2015, edition of *Time* featured a black-and-white image of protests taking place in Baltimore due to the arrest and death of Freddie Gray. white wording on the photo read, "America, ~~1968~~–2015." At first glance and without proper context, the photo looked like it could have been taken in the 1960s. Students of American history know that 1968 was a particularly traumatic year in America. In that year alone, the spring brought about the deaths of both Dr. Martin Luther King Jr. and Sen. Robert Kennedy. The death of the former was likely the impetus behind the selection of the cover photo, as his was also a death that resulted in protests and unrest. There, in 2015, once more was the scene of a tense situation with racial strife at its foundation. The same *Time* photo appeared during the last week of May 2020, except this time both 1968 and 2015 were crossed out leaving 2020. The message: 2020 is revealing some of the same problems that existed in 1968.

I'm of the belief that the world of 2020 is a promising one for millennials like myself. For most of us, our professional lives have kicked into high gear, and we're uniquely positioned to enjoy relationships with both our older generation X peers and our baby boomer parents and grandparents. The latter take pride in reminding us of the differences between the present day and past times like the 1960s. Yet for all the ways 2020 looks and feels different than 1968, some things, including the basic leadership elements that govern the world, seem to remain. One of those elements, courtesy of the Hebrew scriptures, is the continuing roles of prince, priest, and prophet in society. So too, at least in America, remain the symptoms of systemic racism. For literally 401 years, America has kicked the can of unequal treatment of people of African descent down the road.

When these biblical roles are described they are presented as king, priest, and prophet, but for purposes of alliteration, the role of prince in this book is synonymous with the role of king. One, I make no apologies for favoring alliteration, particularly as a black preacher. Two, I don't believe I'm the first to embrace the term *prince* to describe a focal point of civil or political leadership. It was actually the great political theorist Niccolò Machiavelli who famously used the term *prince* to describe the chiefs of sixteenth-century domains in Europe. And then, of course, for many children the concept of a prince is the son of a king. Merriam-Webster also supports my use of this term, defining a prince as "a monarch or king; the ruler of a principality or state."[1]

When the framers laid the foundation of the American government, they intentionally shied away from anything that resembled a monarchy. The Constitution they wrote and ratified assigns the first and largest Article to the legislature, not the executive. Nevertheless, there is an executive, and that executive branch and all it encompasses constitutes our modern prince. What then shall we say about the roles of priest and prophet? The priesthood, the church, the faith community, the religious-industrial complex is just as active as it has ever been, but not necessarily as effective.

The prophetic voice is the one that is far too often missing in action.

This book is not intended to be a literary sermon for library shelves, nor is it intended to join the ranks of the contemporary works of those like Cornel West (who I have much respect for) and others who took to critiquing a president, namely Barack Obama, at every turn. This book is intended to examine the question, What and where is the prophetic leadership in America? And to express just how much it is needed. This question is particularly salient given the breaking-point murder of George Floyd and the more historical rising racial tensions of the final Obama years. Keep in mind the latter occurred in the wake of what was supposed to be a post-racial election of 2008. I'll be the first to admit that statistics clearly state the decline in American religious participation, but that doesn't take away from the knowledge that the priesthood—that is, formal American religion—is active and influential. The prophetic, the forces of society that not only challenge the prince and the priest, but also that do so effectively, is a position that wanted ads all over the nation should be displaying. Or maybe they shouldn't, given the difficulty of that assignment.

Now, just as in the past, abide these three, the prince, the priest, and the prophet. The Hebrew scriptures present us with an image of a God who intended for his chosen people to be led by prophetic leadership only, but their exposure to other nations, and subsequent envy, led them to petition their God through their prophet for monarchical leadership. I used to dismiss the issue of the chosen people asking for a king as just another byproduct of a rebellious spirit. But I think over time I've come to understand that the true detriment of their request lies in the rejection of what their God had for them. The three roles described in this book are universal, even seen in the Christian trinity. Orthodox Christian theology holds that at the foundation of the world there were the Father, the Son, and the Holy Spirit. The Father might be thought of as the eternal prince or ruler of all, and the Son might be viewed as the divine priest who is said to now be "at the right hand of the father making intercessions."[2] Last is the prophetic element of the trinity, the Holy Spirit, the *pneuma*, or breath of God. The end of the word *prophet* is derived from the Latin *phetes* or "speaker." Etymologically, the word *prophet* literally reflects that one cannot speak without breath. Prophets need the breath of God to prophesy. For that reason, it's almost as if in asking for a king, the Israelites were denying, most catastrophically, not only God's breath but God's very sovereignty. With righteous prophets the people had guidance directly from the heart of God, but with the kings the people had directions directly from the heart of humans. The remaining portions of the Old Testament present images of the problems that ensue after God gives the people what they asked for.

I know where I stand on some of the highly publicized tragedies that have befallen America in recent years, and I used to be willing to acknowledge that reasonable individuals can and will always share different perspectives on the root causes of those tragedies. I no longer share that viewpoint. I am now firmly resolved that no reasonable individual could look at the totality of the drama and conclude anything other than "America has a problem with systemic racism." For the sake of our nation we must agree not only that they are tragedies, but that there is an underlying problem that leads to those tragedies. I'm referring to events like the death of Trayvon Martin, who peacefully left a convenience store only to be shot dead. I'm referring to the deaths of Michael Brown and Eric Garner. I speak of the deaths of Tamir Rice, Walter Scott, Freddie Gray, Laquan McDonald, and Sandra Bland. I'm talking about the deaths of Ahmaud Arbery, Breonna Taylor, and of course, George Floyd. I'm pointing out for you the recurring situations in which individuals of color—and by proxy the communities they represent—are seemingly denied justice. I also don't apologize for focusing on systemic racism, as that is America's original sin. There are many isms that could be elevated, but this book is written through my lens as a black man in America focusing on the race problem.

If there was ever a time for prophetic leadership to be on display, it's now. One could discuss prophetic leadership from any number of angles, but my aim is to speak specifically to the issues of racial strife and division that plague us. The statistics don't lie; the responses to questions and individuals tell the truth: America still has a race problem. As recently as 2019, 56% of white and 71% of black Americans said that race relations in the United States were generally bad.[3] I offer that the bigger problem is the lack of prophetic leadership that is willing to speak truth to power. One of the ironies of that May 2015 *Time* cover was that in 1968 among the men killed was a prophetic leader. Few leaders in American history, white or black, reached the level of prophetic influence achieved by the Rev. Dr. Martin Luther King Jr., but it's not the streets, schools, and plazas bearing his name that validate his prophetic contribution. It was the radical king, the non-sanitized and more controversial King, whose words, some fifty-one years after his assassination, still hold truth. King is but one example, who happens to be black, of the prophetic tradition in America. Others like Malcolm X, and even Tupac have offered similar prophetic contributions over time. Yet it is the case that in America our prophets are almost never appreciated in this life. Not only are they without appropriate honor in their own homeland, but they are without appropriate honor in their lifetimes.

Before we can truly progress as a nation—which I believe we will—we must make room for a new generation of prophetic leaders. Sure, access to a pulpit and the strong communication skills needed for effective preaching usually help one's prophetic cause, but our prophetic leaders don't have to be preachers, and many aren't. A prophetic leader can be anyone who speaks truth to power and challenges both the prince and the priests to embrace justice and righteousness. Here, in 2020, we need prophets, and throughout this work, I attempt to make the case that the prophetic voice has been diluted for some time.

In part one of the book I discuss the prince and attempt to analyze what America had in the leadership of Barack Obama. I begin with the circumstances preceding his election and go on to discuss the ways in which his ascension was a response to the times we were experiencing as a nation. I end part one by examining some of the things that, for better or for worse, distinguished President Obama's time in office. Part two discusses the priesthood, the church. This section of the book begins with a review of the Levitical story of Nadab and Abihu, the priestly sons whose illegal sacrifice led to their death. From that story, I move on to discuss black preaching and its musicality. black preaching is relevant because it is the most important element of black worship. In my discussion of the priesthood, I review President Obama's turbulent relationship with the black church going back to the Jeremiah Wright controversy during his first presidential campaign. I move on to discuss President Obama's most beautiful moment related to the black church, and I finish part two by highlighting the realities of two priesthoods, one historically black and the other historically white. In the last section of the book, I discuss the need for (and absence of) the prophetic voice in our nation. I begin this by describing the current president's role in the prophetic conversation. I move on to discuss the game changer that was the burning of Florissant Road in Ferguson, Missouri. The most significant portion of part three is my examination of a few of the symptoms of prophetic lack, and the lack of justice. I move on to posit some thoughts about what we might see President Obama display during his postpresidency work.

I want to acknowledge at the outset that I've been accused of preaching in talking. I can even recall several times over my career that students have said, "Amen," during lessons that obviously had nothing to do with the Gospel. I said that to say, some of this work may read like a sermon, and honestly, I make no apologies for that. I am an unabashed public theologian. I have infused into the work the language of the texts that guide my faith, throughout each section, and in every chapter. However, the goal of the invocation of biblical language is not to proselytize, but rather to provide a framework for the paradigm I have presented. At the same time, I have also undertaken what I believe to be legitimate scholarship and critical analysis. Prayerfully, these components have produced a book worth reading and thoughts worth considering.

Part I
The Prince

CHOOSING SAUL

In social studies, American children learn that the United States has a democratic form of government. From the very beginning, our nation's founders wanted nothing to do with a monarchy. In America, we do have a prince, but the prince isn't a king or a tsar, it's our democratically elected president. There can be no discussion of our prince equivalent without also considering the elections that help us choose the prince. Elections have always fascinated me. I've participated in enough of them to know that elections are both exciting and consequential. America is what it is today because of the results of successive elections. The selection of leadership is fascinating, period, regardless of the method. There is just something very telling about the way a group of people chooses their leaders, especially when circumstances later reveal that they may have chosen the wrong leader. Sometimes the people neglect to approach leadership selection appropriately, and when that happens the results can be catastrophic.

Before I go further, I have to make it clear that in no way am I suggesting that the electorate's choice of Barack H. Obama was a mistake—quite the opposite. I fully believe President Obama was the man for the time, especially given all that our nation had been through under the previous administration. After September 11, Hurricane Katrina, and what was clearly emerging as a recession, it was fitting that we would choose a candidate who represented progress and optimism, and at the time, that was Obama, not his Republican opponent Sen. John McCain.

Even when the right leadership is chosen, the leader or leaders are already handicapped at the onset of their tenure if the people they govern have unrealistic and/or unethical expectations of them. The Obama presidency was plagued by unrealistic expectations. But one expectation that should never be unrealistic is for leaders and the systems they conduct to protect the people. In America our prince is our president, and that individual is the symbolic focal point of our government.

Every year that I taught sixth-grade social studies, I taught a lesson in which I reviewed seven or so of the basic types of government. At some point during the lesson I would have a conversation with my students about the role of government, and one of my savvy students would correctly offer that the role of government is "to protect the people and their property." Officially, definitions of government reference "control," but that control should always be for the purpose of protection. I would continue the discussion with my sixth graders by asking those who had two or more siblings to raise their hands. When hands were raised, I would ask them what conditions would be like in their homes if their parents or guardians were to suddenly leave without notice, and why they'd be that way. Without fail, responses would include terms like *chaos, fighting, no rules,* etc. Even without the full language to express it, my students understood government at the simplest level. As the princes and princesses of their households, mothers and fathers regulate, but they do so to protect the home, both the people and the property.

America in 2020 is not lacking for regulation. Regulation greets us on every street in the form of speed limit signs, and in every workplace in the form of occupational safety standards. We have a lot of regulation, and the more libertarian members of our communities believe that we have too much regulation. Most of us tend to take a more moderate approach because we know that there are some areas of life in which too much regulation can defeat the purpose of a thing. There is, however, another extreme that is best observed through the growing income and wealth disparities in our country. In 2011, a Tumblr page created by members of the Occupy movement popularized a conversation about the 1 percent and the 99 percent, that is the 1 percent of the country with an unbelievable amount of wealth and the 99 percent constituting everyone else.[1] The exchange about wealth disparity is still happening, and such percentage talk was frequently referenced by candidates in the 2020 presidential election cycle.[2] More than just being a discussion, that conversation spoke to the bona fide reality that problems arise when *economic* regulation is lacking. Finding the right regulatory balance is hard, and in America it happens via a process of political tug-of-war. On either side of that rope are needs and wants. As developed as humans are, we as a species seem to struggle with the balance between what is essential for our survival and what fulfills us in a given moment. It is hard for a population—remember democracy is supposed to be government by the population—to see beyond the present. In a democracy such as ours, wants typically defeat needs.

The People Get What They Want

The biblical narrative of Saul presented in the book of 1 Samuel both highlights the error of elevating wants above needs and reinforces the importance of having a prince to protect the people. In the Bible, Saul was the famous Israelite predecessor of King David; in fact, Saul was Israel's very first king. Saul's rise was little more than the consequence of height and stature. When we look at the history of Saul, we don't find him having many of the qualifications that should define strong leaders.

Later in the biblical narrative, before David, the eighth and youngest son of a man named Jesse, was chosen to be king, the Bible tells of how David's history includes wrestling matches with lions and bears. We are told that David had defended his father's property (sheep) valiantly against savage animals, and there's also a story about David defeating a huge giant named Goliath when no one else was willing to fight him. Before David even assumed power, the masses he would eventually rule had this chant on their lips:

> *Saul has killed his thousands*
> *David has killed his ten thousands*[3]

Based on that chant alone, David seemed to be at least a *reasonable* choice to succeed king Saul, even though he lacked the royal blood of Saul's own children. Despite having grown up with what many considered to be a soft demeanor, David had already proven at his young age that he was brave and at least somewhat competent in armed conflict.

One other line in the story of Saul has always caught my attention. When it was time for the people to ratify the God-given choice of Saul as leader, they initially couldn't find him. When they finally did find their new king, Saul was hiding in what King James translators called "the stuff."[4] More modern translations have used words like baggage, or equipment, but the word *stuff* is probably the most powerful word that can be used in that verse. Here, then, is just one concern with the ascension of Saul. Even though the people needed regulation and protection, a fact God had never denied, their preference for the instrument of regulation and governance was the wrong one. Their first king was not a tested warrior, he was not an experienced elder of the community, nor was he a successful merchant or farmer. Saul was nothing but a tall, strong, and by all accounts, handsome man. Not only that, but on inauguration day, Saul was not found standing with his inaugural speech in hand confidently displaying the swag befitting his stature. Instead, Saul was found hiding in a pile of stuff. Before proceeding, let that sink in.

To be clear, the text does say that God specifically instructed Samuel to anoint Saul as king, but the text is also clear that the people were demanding a king and would settle for nothing less.[5] It has long seemed to me like the only reason God instructed Samuel to choose Saul was because he understood that unless the prophet presented a tall and handsome man, the people would not follow their new leader. For the people, the idea of leadership was wrapped up in a look. It's no wonder that years later when it came time to anoint Saul's successor, God had to remind the same prophet, "The Lord does not see as mortals see; they look on the outward appearance, but the Lord looks on the heart."[6]

Choosing an American Prince

We have to take a step back and think through how Saul arrived at his moment of elevation. Saul himself was not the problem; the process that led to Saul's selection was the problem. The biblical account in 1 Samuel expresses that the God of the Israelites never intended for his chosen people to be ruled via monarchy. Nevertheless, in God's permissive will, the requests of the Israelites were granted, and they received their king. To set them up for possible success, God chose a king they would be likely to follow, one who looked like a monarch and who looked as though he could go before them in battle. This was a king who, standing head and shoulders above everyone else around him, should've been able to make them victorious against their chief struggles, primarily manifested in the form of warring nations like the Philistines.

If you're like me, you can see some parallels between the ascension of Saul and that of Barack Obama. By nature of being the first African American president, Barack Obama will always be considered a historic and transformational American leader. I could spend pages here in Obama apologetics, defending his accomplishments, of which I am the first to admit he had many. Yet as we find with Saul, I can't help but believe that in many of his most challenging circumstances, President Obama himself was not the problem. The problem was the process by which he was chosen to be the leader. It can never be a good thing when leaders are selected for the wrong reasons or with the wrong expectations, even if they are the right leaders. I cannot overemphasize that my personal belief is that Barack Obama was the right leader for 2008, and the eight years after, but that doesn't negate the fact that he was partially selected for the wrong reasons, chief among them being that he was the opposite of George W. Bush.

I can recall very well the presidential primary debates of 2008 during which there was little substantive policy difference between then-Senators Obama and Clinton. Probably the most significant area of difference was Senator Clinton's vote to authorize the Iraq War. Even though he was not serving in Congress at the time, prior to the Iraq War then-Illinois state senator Barack Obama was on record opposing the authorization of force in Iraq. Senator Clinton, on the other hand, voted for it, and that vote was just the opening that Barack Obama needed to eventually win the Democratic presidential nomination. Obama was able to capitalize on the anti-war sentiment in the country. That sentiment ultimately helped propel him to the White House. Even more than that was the fact that he represented hope. Hope and change, but mostly hope. The hope that Obama represented was iconized in a now-famous HOPE poster by artist Shepard Fairey. There was hope that America's economy could be turned around;

hope that we could progress toward a post-racial society (which in hindsight sounds ignorant on many levels); hope that America was going to leave almost a decade of military engagement behind us. And last but not least, hope that a long wish list of progressive agenda items was finally going to materialize, including universal healthcare. There was indeed hope, but like everything else, hope must eventually face reality.

Waiving Our Rights

Before anyone can fully consider the role of the American prince, they have to consider the framework in which the American prince operates. Our process for selecting leaders has been influenced by Western political theory and philosophy. The system in which the president governs is influenced by the same schools of thought. Several of Western thought's most impactful social philosophers examined what we now know as the *law of nature*, or alternatively, *natural law*. Each of these philosophers found that a natural, God-given code existed which was supposed to allow humans to be born equal, but also give those same humans the ability to act in ways that could harm society. John Locke and Thomas Hobbes were just two of those philosophers who identified the negative aspects of natural law. Both of them had a prescribed form of government that they believed was the best way to counter the possible harm that could arise with natural law. In actuality, both also displayed contradictions within their arguments, and as such, the systems of government they suggested ended up being incompatible with their assessments of the law of nature.

Mr. Locke acknowledged that humans were inherently biased in their decision-making due to their personal property interests, but he believed a democratic system of government would have enough checks in it to overcome that particular flaw. Mr. Hobbes identified a natural human tendency toward war, but he believed that a single sovereign human, even with their own insecurities, could somehow provide security for the rest of society.

Let me here explain why it's worth it to wax philosophical. I've turned to political philosophy to highlight the X factor in every conversation about leadership: human nature. Many of us have a tendency to forget the humanity of leaders, regardless of whether it is the parent we expect to be a superhero, the pastor we forget is made of the same sinful flesh as us, or, perhaps most consequentially, the president we expect to fix all of the problems in the country. The late theologian Robert W. Jenson acknowledged such a tendency in the American psyche specifically: Most societies have put a man, a being who can love and be loved, at the center: the sovereign, the Fürher, the divine hero. This is much the older and more usual way; and also America's unofficial institutions testified to its attraction— if our president or his wife has the slightest hint of royal manner or distinction, we become slavish in our devotion; and if there is war or other emergency, all parties proclaim "uniting behind the president" as our highest duty, even if that particular president is an unlikely bearer of national moral purpose.[7]

To make the message clearer, in the moment it might seem like the potential first black president can eradicate racism in a country that was built on it, but with the sobriety of reflection we realize that said individual is just a limited human like the rest of us. We forget that the law of nature even applies to our leaders, especially our princes. That's why the law of nature is germane to considerations about the formation of a democratic government. Both Locke and Hobbes understood this.

Each of these English philosophers thought about human nature as they theorized the type of government that might work best. They agreed that the freedom and liberty humans have gained through nature should be regulated, but held different views on how to do so.

Locke implied at length that government really existed to regulate property, but he also understood that the regulation of property wasn't a simple matter. Regulation had to extend to the labor needed to improve the property, as well as consideration of whether or not the property was an overall asset or liability to the general population. Locke acknowledged that under the law of nature, humans were born equal and asserted that it was through our labor and the acquisition (and even improvement) of property that we begin to see groupings or classes in society. Locke believed that the same law of nature that created equal humans also allowed them to become selfish. Taking all of those things into account—and that is a lot to take into account—Locke suggested that a *democratic* system be created to allow the community to stem the tide of any selfish objectives. That is to say, a system in which accountability didn't rest in any one potentially selfish person, but in the people as a whole. For surely—with just a hint of sarcasm—in a democracy, selfish motives would never win the day.

Concerning an appropriate type of government, Hobbes arrived at a completely different conclusion. He recognized that power was an important element in the working of society and believed that there needed to be a sovereign authority in government to enforce laws. The sovereign, according to Hobbes, was supposed to make the laws in the name of the people. In order to make laws, the sovereign needed to have the power to do so. Hobbes concluded that true power was in *the exercise* of power. In other words the sovereign's power could only be as strong as their ability to persuade the citizens to do as they desired. A conflict arises when Hobbes's view on the law of nature is considered in the context of the system he advocated for. Hobbes wrote that each man has the liberty "to use his own power as he wills himself" but modified that view by implying that rights should be waived for the good of the state.[8]

Honestly, the issue for me with Hobbes has always been that unless there is complete anarchy, any people with any type of government are already waiving rights simply by having a government. There can be no prince, president, premier, etc. without the waiving of rights. Maybe that's why the prophet Samuel warned those requesting a king:

> These will be the ways of the king who will reign over you: he will take your sons and appoint them to his chariots and to be his horsemen, and to run before his chariots; and he will appoint for himself commanders of thousands and commanders of fifties, and some to plow his ground and to reap his harvest, and to make his implements of war and the equipment of his chariots. He will take your daughters to be perfumers and cooks and bakers. He will take the best of your fields and vineyards and olive orchards and give them to his courtiers. He will take one-tenth of your grain and of your vineyards and give it to his officers and his courtiers. He will take your male and female slaves, and the best of your cattle and donkeys, and put them to his work. He will take one-tenth of your flocks, and you shall be his slaves.[9]

The Hobbesian view was that in waiving natural rights to the sovereign, each person could endeavor to keep society in a state of peace. If rights were not waived, society would be in a state of perpetual war, since each man's natural rights would somehow be in conflict with the natural rights of everyone else. It was only through the waiving of rights that a legitimate sovereign could be established. Yet, lest we think that Hobbes wanted a free-for-all where the people were passive subjects to any kind of leadership, there was a caveat: the sovereign was supposed to act justly. That meant the sovereign needed to waive some of their own rights to ensure that peace was maintained in society. Even where there was a prince, the prince still had a responsibility to do the right thing. This is an important point that we'll revisit in a second.

In the meantime, here's where things get a little tricky, at least for a Pentecostal preacher like me. Locke's view on the law of nature was tied up in his view of reason. For him, it was reason that allowed people to live peaceably with one another. He suggested that everyone was free and was allotted the same amount of power in the form of human capacity. Any individual could use their capacity to obtain property, and even labor on that property. Human capacity allowed one to improve his or her natural condition. However, the supposed soundness of any improvements the individual made to their property was based on how well they applied reason. Locke understood reason to be an essential element of the law of nature because even as a man could do good with the liberty he was given, he could also transgress against himself and others. Although all had liberty, no one was supposed to "harm another in life, health, liberty, or possessions" unless they were doing so to apply justice.[10]

Hobbes too viewed the law of nature as giving people basic equality. He stated that this law made man equal. As such, almost all men thought they had greater wisdom than others, whom they considered vulgar. Hobbes saw in men a propensity toward competition and glory, both of which led to distrust of others' abilities. Both Lock and Hobbes maintained that the law of nature made men equal, but they also shared a pessimistic view of the human capacity to keep the peace. They saw man's life on Earth as solitary and short. Hobbes believed the natural condition was every man existing as an enemy to every other man, because there was no greater security. With such conditions the natural end could only be war. Hobbes, concerned about man's susceptibility to war, was convinced that a strong sovereign, for our purposes a strong prince, was the only capable way to provide the security that the natural condition alone would deny.

Although Locke recognized human bias to be inherent in the law of nature, he made the claim that a democratic legislature was the best way to deal with it. Locke believed that a democratic state would be composed of individuals who consent to a community that makes decisions (primarily regarding property). The community would collectively decide the use and value of property. This was why the government existed, at least for Locke, to regulate property. Today, though, we can't possibly see Locke's assertions as reasonable either. Rather than checking the personal biases of a community of individuals, the biases of those making the decisions influence the decisions. That's why today most property decisions are the result of personal biases. I've seen this firsthand as a local school board member, making decisions that I hope are in the best interest of the community and its schools. I like to think I'm a good person who always votes objectively, but do I have biases? Absolutely. Do the other eight school board members have them? Without a doubt! I understand that Locke believed property decisions should be made with the consent of the majority, but there was and is nothing to prevent the majority from having biased views. At the end of the day people tend toward protecting their interests, which are invariably tied to their property. That is, if we're just considering *nature*.

Hobbes suggested that every man be willing to lay down his rights to try and strive for the peace of all. He also believed that inherent in the human nature was an insecurity about one's self and possessions. For that reason, he expressed a belief that the best way to compensate for that natural insecurity was for the members of society to collectively yield their rights to a sovereign, empowering that individual to provide their security. That belief, too, was flawed, simply because the sovereign himself was a human struggling with the natural condition. Applying Hobbes's belief of the natural condition, there was no possible way that the sovereign alone could deal with both their insecurities and the insecurities of society as a whole. To further exacerbate the flaw in Hobbes's thinking, Hobbes suggested that the sovereign should not only be empowered to enforce the laws, but that he should also be empowered to make the laws. He stated, "If a monarch . . . grants a liberty to all or any of his subjects, but this grant disables the sovereign from providing for the safety of the subjects, the grant is void."[11] If the sovereign was vested with power, power then would become a personal possession of the sovereign, and he, like his subjects, would seek to maintain and secure *his* personal possession. The insecurity of the sovereign's power would lead him to govern in a way that emphasized the maintenance of power rather than the effective use of it. In modern vernacular, we'd use the proverbial saying from nineteenth-century British politician Lord Acton, "Absolute power corrupts absolutely."[12]

The summary is that Locke tended toward the influence of reason, and Hobbes tended toward the influence of passions. Both philosophers identified a natural existence in which all humans enter life with the same capacity. Yet each saw within that natural existence human capacity leading to negative ends, with Hobbes presenting the more pessimistic of the two views. Locke saw democratic governance as the best way to govern the variable part of the human existence—property. Hobbes believed that a strong sovereign could control most if not all aspects of the state. If you ask me, both philosophers contradicted their views of the law of nature. Locke failed to acknowledge the personal biases of those he would invest with power. Hobbes failed to acknowledge the insecurity of the sovereign that he would have to rule the state. In neglecting to account for their own assessments of human nature, each philosopher presented a polity that was destined to fail at some point.

And therein lies the important truth: in our own capacity, we are all destined to fail at some point. Notice I said *in our own capacity*. In human nature, failure is inherent, either because of personal biases or personal insecurities. That's why so many of us ground our work in a higher power, because we have been convinced that to do anything less is to by default head toward failure. So it is for us; so it is for the prince.

Saul Was Anointed

Make no mistake, the biblical account is clear that Saul was the anointed prince for the people of Israel. Saul was the one who the prophet Samuel had anointed. Saul was the one who God had given to the people. The biblical narrative tells of how Saul was promised signs to prove that God was with him as the anointed leader, the final one of which was that Saul would be transformed in a prophetic way:

> Then you shall go on from there further and come to the oak of Tabor; three men going up to God at Bethel will meet you there, one carrying three kids, another carrying three loaves of bread, and another carrying a skin of wine. They will greet you and give you two loaves of bread, which you shall accept from them. After that you shall come to Gibeath-elohim, at the place where the Philistine garrison is; there, as you come to the town, you will meet a band of prophets coming down from the shrine with harp, tambourine, flute, and lyre playing in front of them; they will be in a prophetic frenzy. Then the spirit of the Lord will possess you, and you will be in a prophetic frenzy along with them and be turned into a different person. Now when these signs

meet you, do whatever you see fit to do, for God is with you.[13]

The message from the prophet for the newly anointed prince was that as confirmation of his new office, he would actually *prophesy*. More than that, he would also be turned into a different person, because one cannot truly speak prophetically without being transformed by the spirit with which they speak. The text of 1 Samuel doesn't offer an account of what Saul said when he prophesied, or how he prophesied. Neither does it say that in that moment he held the office of prophet. The text simply states that he prophesied, and we know that the people he would soon lead recognized that something about him was different:

> When they were going from there to Gibeah, a band of prophets met him; and the spirit of God possessed him, and he fell into a prophetic frenzy along with them. When all who knew him before saw how he prophesied with the prophets, the people said to one another, "What has come over the son of Kish? Is Saul also among the prophets?"[14]

Looking back on it, it is amazing just how naïve a whole country can be when it is caught up in the fervor of the moment. Hope can have that sort of effect on people. Hope can be so intoxicating that it can cause whole groups of people to put blinders on. I'm a big Star Wars fan, and in the franchise, Luke Skywalker was the "New Hope" after years of an Evil Empire ruling the galaxy. In 1988 Jesse Jackson told America to "keep hope alive," and in 2008 America had a skinny guy with big ears from Chicago telling America about the "audacity of hope." What exactly were we supposed to have the audacity to hope for? If we were to ask, I would bet that a whole lot of Americans who were alive in 2008 really don't know what they were supposed to be hoping for, but they hoped nonetheless.

I'll admit, I was young in the 1990s, so anything I say about the 1990s is colored by youth. However, even in my youth, I was a witness to the change that happened by the time 2008 rolled around, and it was clear to me that something in America was just different. Maybe I can pinpoint the change to September 11, 2001. That day changed more than just travel plans; it reoriented our politics. The immediate aftermath of September 11 propelled George W. Bush to 80 percent approval in the public and suddenly thrust our nation on a path to war. It shouldn't be too much of a stretch then to say there likely would've never been an election of Barack Obama in 2008 if there was no reelection of George W. Bush in 2004.

THE PREVIOUS PRINCE

On July 27, 2004 millions around the world watched Illinois state senator Barack H. Obama deliver the Democratic National Convention keynote speech, and that moment, a magical one, would catapult him onto the national political scene. Also in 2004, through a convergence of factors, America reelected George W. Bush and initiated the sequence of events that resulted in the election of the first black president.

The 2004 presidential election was historic for any number of reasons, but high among them was the outsized impact of religion on our politics. At the time we were in the middle of the Iraq War, which had started as a popular invasion, but over time deteriorated into a quagmire. The 2004 presidential election was also the first one in the post-September 11 world. Those terrorist attacks were fresh in the minds of many Americans, and that along with the ongoing military offensive in Afghanistan brought national security issues to the political forefront. It also paved the way for Republican strategists to make a religious appeal to the electorate and to use wedge issues to exploit the religiosity of many voters. In 2004 it was the Republican Party that benefitted from a sort of fear that lingered in the nation—they did so again in 2016.

The Context of 2004

In 2000 George W. Bush lost the popular vote but secured the presidency via the electoral college. After that popular vote loss, Republicans, led by Bush's chief strategist Karl Rove, designed a strategy built around strong turnout from people of faith. The Republican Party understood that they had cultural conservatives on their side. The challenge was to entice those voters to the polls. For them, the way to do that was by forcing religion to the front of the issues radar, especially with opposition to same-sex marriage, abortion, and other hot-button social issues. On the other side, the Democratic Party had no choice but to moderate its platform for fear of losing too many cultural conservatives. The result was an election in which both religious activists and their opponents were emboldened into action. Ultimately, religion benefited the Republican nominee, and the Democratic nominee was unable to carry even most Catholic voters, those from his own denominational affiliation. The competitive battleground victories that enabled the reelection of George W. Bush were largely a result of the support he enjoyed from one group: religious conservatives.

To fully understand how the politics of religion in 2004 connect to the election of Barack Obama in 2008, we have to consider the war— the Iraq War. It's hard to overstate how the ongoing offensive in Iraq dominated the 2004 election. The Iraq War went on for years, but it officially started with an initial invasion on March 20, 2003. Until taking time to reflect, I never really connected the dots, but as time has passed a clearer narrative has developed. Eventually one can see how the night vision images of missiles in March 2003 were a part of the political rise of Barack Obama. I actually remember watching the breaking news as coalition troops initiated a "shock and awe" campaign, full of flashing lights and repetitive booms. The Iraq War complicated the electorate's choice because the incumbent, President

Bush, successfully made the case that switching commander-in-chief in the middle of the war was dangerous. And while Bush's opponent, John Kerry, touted his firsthand experience as a decorated Vietnam Veteran, it didn't have the same impact. The war was growing costlier and more unpopular by the day, yet Kerry was even openly opposed by many of his fellow veterans for his strong antiwar stance and apparent indiscretions toward veterans after returning home from Vietnam—Vietnam was forty years prior.

The Iraq War was an outgrowth of the War on Terror which began after the terrorist attacks of September 11, 2001. Following that fateful day, the Bush administration made fighting terrorism its top priority, and soon after initiated an offensive against the Taliban in Afghanistan. That offensive had popular support, and many viewed it as successful. Even with war still raging in Afghanistan, the Bush administration soon began an unrelenting effort to fight terrorism on a broader scale. Iraqi president Saddam Hussein was an easy target. He had antagonized the US going back to the first Bush administration, and Americans were used to seeing infrared-vision images of strikes on Iraq throughout the '90s. Only a decade and a half prior to the Iraq War, Americans had witnessed an entire war (the Gulf War) waged against Iraq. With public support high, the Bush administration had relative ease selling the Iraq War to the American public, especially with trusted and tested political figures like secretary of state Colin Powell making the case.

Iraq and Afghanistan were home to two simultaneous wars being waged by the United States, and the political climate created by those wars contributed to an atmosphere of unease about the direction of the country, as well as a spirit of fear that the Republican Party was able to connect to social issues. Political scientist Larry Sabato wrote that "the biggest 'religion' story of the [2004] campaign was how national security was tied to faith either directly or via 'moral' values."[1] There were exit polls that revealed that some groups, particularly women (especially religious women), were key in deciding the outcome of the election. This group had an apparent fear of a second terrorist attack, and that fear is a prime example of the things weighing on the minds of voters at the time. Fear emboldened both religious activists and their opponents into participation in the election.

It's interesting to contrast the fear driving the 2004 election with the hope driving the 2008 election. It's even more interesting to contrast the hope of 2008 with the fears at the center of the 2016 election. One begins to see the interweaving between fear, hope, and America's electoral outcomes. In 2004, fears abounded. In addition to the general fears about terrorism, religious voters in particular had unease about so-called activist judges. It seems absurd in 2020 as a conservative supreme court continues to undo years of progress, but at the time the term *activist* was really "code for abortion, gay rights, and limits on establishment of religion."[2]

Religion's Role in 2004

The 2004 presidential election represented the most recent shift in the religious dynamics of the electorate, specifically regarding evangelical Christians. There was a New Christian Right that had begun with Ronald Reagan's courting of Christians in 1980, but before Reagan it was Democrat Jimmy Carter who had success in courting Christians.[3] Reagan's effectiveness at courting this group surpassed Carter's. In 1976 Carter waded into religious politics, making it a point to establish himself as a Southern Christian, and famously using the term "born-again" to define his faith. What we now know as the Christian Right continued to gain strength as a political force throughout the 1980s and probably would have continued to strengthen if it weren't for a few obstacles. What were those obstacles? Just several scandals of major televangelists during the late 1980s, as well as the failed presidential bid of one of the Christian Right's leaders, Pat Robertson. These disappointments contributed to the end of a major phase of evangelical political engagement.[4] By 2004 president George W. Bush appeared to be the Religious Right's heir to Reagan. The first president Bush shied away from talking about religion during both of his presidential campaigns and single term in office. George W., however, actively built religious support.

There is no doubt in my mind that George W. Bush was reelected in 2004 because of wedge issues: gay marriage (as it was called then), abortion, stem-cell research, and human cloning. Conservatives exaggerated each of these issues and exploited their importance with the goal of polarizing the electorate. The strategy worked. In 2004, when asked about the most important issue affecting their vote, a plurality of voters chose "moral values."[5] What's impressive is how the Bush reelection team was able to orchestrate a polarized electorate even though they didn't become directly involved in certain issues. For example, on the issue of gay marriage, the Bush campaign was reluctant to engage in the debate and chose instead to allow voices in the Christian right to debate the issue for them.[6] As a result, the general election included eleven same-sex marriage ballot initiatives throughout the country, each of which was adopted by double digits in its respective state.[7] That almost seems preposterous sixteen years later, having gone through eight years of a progressive Obama presidency that gave the LGBTQ community many of the wins they were looking for.

Sure, wedge issues were determining factors in how votes were cast, but religion was on the mind of the electorate for other reasons as well. Mel Gibson's *The Passion of the Christ* had just been released the previous February. It forced the nation to think about religion and emboldened many Christians to represent their faith. On the other side, events like Janet Jackson's wardrobe malfunction during the Super Bowl XXXVIII halftime show, legal challenges to the constitutionality of the Pledge of Allegiance, and a Massachusetts Supreme Court ruling in favor of same-sex marriage angered many religious voters. Angering such an energized segment of the electorate was significant because in 2004, a voter's degree of religiosity dramatically affected how they voted. Voting patterns differed less on the basis of faith and more on the degree to which that faith was practiced.

Before 1972, there was no religion gap between those with regular church attendance and those without it. Such an attendance gap appeared almost out of nowhere in 1972, reached a low in 1988, suddenly widened again in 1992, and then peaked during the 2004 election.[8] By 2004, overall church attendance in the US had fallen to 42 percent from 49 percent in the 1960s.[9] A June 2004 Gallup poll revealed that "60 percent of Americans thought religion was a 'very important' part of their lives and thought that religion could answer all or most of society's problems."[10] That meant that any candidate who could exploit the religiosity of the electorate was in a position to do really well in the election. For many voters, religion was not only an important part of their lives but expected to be an important part of the life of the candidate they supported. That was just another way Bush and the Republican Party were positioned to benefit. Bush won 91 percent of voters who thought that the most important quality in a candidate was religious faith.[11]

Political Party Approaches to Religion in 2004

The two major political parties responded differently to the heightened importance of religion during the 2004 campaign, but they both recognized it and attempted early on to exploit it for votes. Take, for instance, former Vermont governor and Democratic Party chair Howard Dean, who did not win the Democratic nomination. Many believe that Dean lost the Democratic nomination partly because he was viewed as too secular to win in certain parts of the country.[12] During his primary campaign, Dean recognized that his lack of religion was a problem, and several times he attempted to remedy the problem. In one specific instance, he called former president Jimmy Carter to ask if he could attend services at Carter's church in Georgia for a photo op.[13] Voters saw through it and still see through those kinds of cheap attempts to pander.

Like many of his Democratic primary opponents, the eventual Democratic nominee, John Kerry, struggled to navigate the politics of religion. Nevertheless, Kerry's campaign recognized that religion mattered and like the Republicans, tried its best to exploit the issue. Kerry had both personal and policy struggles with religion. Although he identified as Catholic and tried to use his Catholicism to his advantage, he was not able to turn his faith into an asset. He attended an unconventional Catholic church in Boston called the Paulist Center, which *The New York Times* described as "a nontraditional, New Age-oriented church."[14] Kerry's church represented a kind of liberal Catholicism that most Catholics were uncomfortable with. In all actuality, Kerry was uncomfortable with religion in general and produced gaffes when speaking about religious topics. On one occasion he stated, "My oath privately between me and God was defined in the Catholic church by Pius XXIII and Pope Paul VI in the Vatican II." Here's what made that a gaffe: no Pope Pius XXIII has ever existed.[15] Kerry's attempts to exploit religion to his benefit began around July 2004, with increased efforts to highlight moral values on the campaign trail. As the winner of the Democratic primary, he had the ability to influence the party platform, and the final draft of the platform mentioned God five times.[16] After the conventions, Kerry attempted to use the presidential debates to gain headway on the issue of religion but was unsuccessful. In the second debate—held town hall style—Kerry began his response to a question about government-funded abortion by talking about his Catholic upbringing, being an altar boy, and his faith sustaining him in Vietnam.[17] Unfortunately for Kerry the public's perception of him as a candidate lacking a core of faith lingered, and he was unable to use religion to his benefit. Like so many politicians, in the closing months of the campaign, Kerry made frequent appearances in African American pulpits and even held a nationwide conference call with Bill Clinton to two thousand black clergy just days before the election.[18] It didn't work.

John Kerry discussed religion out of necessity, and it showed. On the other side, like Reagan before him, George W. Bush capitalized on his comfort with the topic. Bush's aim was to win over Christian conservatives, who he considered a prized voting bloc. During the 2004 campaign, PBS produced a documentary titled *The Jesus Factor* that focused on Bush's strong faith. Bush owed his religion strategy to chief strategist and political advisor Karl Rove. Rove was very public with the belief that the Bush campaign could and should make every effort to win over Christian conservatives. One of the more intriguing features of the Bush campaign was the degree to which they were public with their belief about the importance of Christian conservatives to their reelection prospects. Moves like the appointment of conservative John Ashcroft as attorney general, support for constitutional amendments banning gay marriage, vouchers for religious schools, bans on partial-birth abortions, and the elevation of faith-based initiatives were really part of "a four-year effort" on the part of the Bush campaign to win the favor of religiously conservative voters.[19]

Then there were the wedge issues. Rove and the other Bush strategists knew that if certain polarizing issues were elevated, they could spur the most passionate voters (i.e., conservative Christians) to the polls.

Sure, there were multiple wedge issues during the 2004 campaign, but the two most important were abortion and same-sex marriage. Very little had happened on the abortion front over the previous few years, so Republicans made partial-birth abortion the issue. Even more than just energizing a key segment of the electorate, the wedge issues that the Republican Party was so successful at exploiting became representative of deeper-held feelings by conservatives across the country. Gay marriage became the "catchall for concerns about activist courts, banning school prayer, attempts to remove 'under God' from the Pledge of Allegiance, and limiting religious displays in public."[20] Then there was the frequency with which those issues were referenced in the debates, usually to Bush's benefit. Bush was lauded for his clear answers on opposition to abortion in the second debate. In the third debate moderator Bob Schieffer asked Bush if homosexuality was a choice. Bush responded, "I don't know," but went on to say, "As we respect someone's rights . . . we shouldn't change—or have to change— our basic views on the sanctity of marriage."[21] Bush's response won praise from critics for its clarity.

Wedge issues were one part of the Bush strategy, but another was cloaked in the term "faith-based outreach." Such outreach was intended to be a less-divisive way of connecting Bush with religious groups. There were policy elements of this part of the Bush strategy, but also more subtle ways of advancing it. Maybe the best example of this is Bush's response when asked to name his favorite political philosopher. He named Christ.[22] Maybe Bush did sincerely answer the question, but one can also argue the he might have been trying to appeal to evangelical Christians. Richard Land, a leader of the Southern Baptist Convention, was quoted as saying, "This president's heartbeat is close to the heartbeat of Southern Baptists when it comes to the very serious and important public policy issues."[23] Whether or not Land's statement was true, Bush's faith-based approach to campaigning came off as more genuine than his opponent's, and not by a little bit.

The important nuance about 2004 is that the presidential election was less about religion and more about *religiosity*. One's degree of religious adherence was more of a determinant than religious identification, but some patterns emerged among members of particular religious groups. In general, evangelicals, mainline Protestants, and weekly attending Catholics backed Bush in large numbers, while less observant Catholics, Jews, and those of non-Christian faiths generally backed Kerry.[24]

Religious Groups and the 2004 Election

As one might imagine, Christians made up a majority of the electorate in 2004. Much like the electorate, Christianity has become increasingly postdenominational. At one time there were significant electoral differences between individuals from different denominations, but electoral differences are now based on religiosity regardless of which denomination one identifies with. Bush identified as a Protestant Christian (Methodist), which afforded him a luxury that Kerry did not have—Bush was able to avoid denominational discussions. According to Sabato, "By emphasizing his own personal religious experience over his identity as a Methodist, Bush resembled . . . the postdenominational non-doctrinaire Protestantism widespread in contemporary America."[25] Clearly, religion was an important part of

Bush's candidacy; he simply chose to address it from a postdenominational yet Christian standpoint.

The most important group of Christians in the 2004 election were evangelical Christians. Evangelicals came from all Christian denominations. This group had a resurgence with Bush's election in 2000 and were actively courted by the Bush campaign. "Evangelical Protestants" represented 25 percent of the US population in 2004, Catholics 22 percent, and 17 percent were unaffiliated.[26] Evangelicalism is characterized by conservatism not necessarily in the political sense, but in terms of religious practice, doctrine, and belief. Robert E. Denton offered a great summary of the politics of conservative evangelicals, at least in 2004. He said, "Conservative Christians as individuals do not separate their lives into a private and public sphere."[27] So simple yet so important if one is going to understand why conservative Christians have voted the way they've voted. Bush was even able to make some headway with black evangelicals who tended to be socially conservative. In particular, black evangelicals were very wary of Kerry's support of gay marriage, which was an issue that was extremely unpopular in the black community.[28]

The second most important group of Christians in the 2004 election was Catholics. The Catholic vote was split almost evenly between Bush and Kerry, which is interesting considering that Kerry publicly identified as a Catholic. Kerry had a horrible showing among Catholics, which was indicative of the exodus of Catholics from the Democratic base. Catholics were at one time solidly Democratic in voting pattern, but by 2004 there was no longer a "Catholic vote" for either party. At one time Catholics voted more out of tradition and historical connection, but by 2004 Catholics voted more based on individual issues. In 1960, a Catholic Democrat from Massachusetts, John F. Kennedy, took 82 percent of the Catholic vote. In 2004, a Catholic Democrat from Massachusetts, John F. Kerry, took less than 50 percent of it.[29] A July 2004 Pew poll revealed that only 43 percent of American Catholics knew that Kerry was a Catholic.[30] Kerry did little to help himself. As he was on a ski trip in March of 2004, Kerry received the eucharist, or what some of us call holy communion. Kerry received this rite, the most sacred in all of Catholicism, in a ski suit.[31] That episode only fed the perception that he lacked sincerity when it came to his faith. Even if the other 67 percent of Catholics had been aware of Kerry's Catholicism, they probably would have voted the same way based on their issue orientation. From the summer of 2004 until Election Day in November, Bush actually received a 22 percent swing in the Catholic vote, again showing that issues were more important for Catholic voters than party affiliation.[32]

Even with the Catholic vote split between Bush and Kerry, the Catholic establishment was solidly anti-Kerry. In the words of Paul Kengor, "There was concern that a President Kennedy would look to the Pope for guidance . . . there was concern that a President Kerry would take no advice from the Pope."[33] The US Conference of Catholic Bishops published their own guide to the election, *Faithful Citizenship: A Catholic Call to Political Responsibility*, which reinforced the church's conservative stance on many issues.[34] Overall, Catholics were among the most active religious groups in 2004. On the organizing end were pro-Bush efforts like the GOP's website, KerryWrongForCatholics.com, and pro-Kerry groups like Catholics for Free Choice, Catholic Action Network, and Catholics for the Common Good. On the extreme end were Catholic leaders like St. Louis archbishop-designate Raymond Burke, who told priests to refuse communion to elected officials who supported abortion rights. That ban was later extended to Catholics who voted for candidates that backed abortion rights. [35]

Non-Christian groups generally backed Kerry, and in some cases, this was a major change from the 2000 election. In 2000, Bush won a plurality of Muslims, but that dwindled to only 7 percent in 2004.[36] Many have speculated that the dramatic shift in Muslim support was due to the aftermath of September 11 and the wars in Iraq and Afghanistan. On the other hand, Bush improved his share of the Jewish vote, going from 19 percent in 2000 to 25 percent in 2004.[37] That small change may have been related to the lack of a Jewish running mate on the opposing ticket (Joe Lieberman, who practiced Orthodox Judaism, was the 2000 Democratic vice presidential nominee). Non-religious voters were also important in the election. Bush decisively won those who attended religious services at least once a month or more, and Kerry won those who attended services less than monthly.[38]

Among scholars who have studied 2004, there is pretty much universal agreement that religiosity mattered, but there is not unanimity on whether or not it was the deciding factor. In June 2004 reverend Barry Lynn commented that the ongoing election was "rapidly becoming the most religiously infused in modern American history."[39] Rev. Lynn's assertion was supported by the record of increased political activity of religious organizations that year, activity that was both solicited and unsolicited by candidates. Things got so bad that during the campaign the IRS sent letters to both parties to remind them that churches were at risk of losing their tax-exempt status for engaging in political activities.[40] Many outside groups mobilized churches and churchgoers on behalf of the campaigns. As you can probably guess, these activities mostly benefited the Republican Party.

I believe there is a lot of evidence to support the claim that Bush won in 2004 because of his support from conservative voters voting on the basis of religion. An examination of the battleground states alone shows that religion was a pivotal factor in each state. Two-thirds of the battleground states were ones in which Catholicism was the dominant religion.[11] In the states that went to Bush, which included many of those battleground states, Kerry lost the Catholic vote by twenty points.[42] In many of the battleground states, Protestant ministers were marshaled by the Bush campaign to increase voter turnout among their congregations.[43] In Arkansas and West Virginia the Republican National Committee distributed mailings that implied a Democratic win would lead to the "banning of the Bible."[44] In the Midwest, Christian conservatives were motivated by the wedge issues that were so prevalent during the campaign, including opposition to abortion and opposition to gay marriage. It is entirely plausible that their increased turnout put Bush over the top in some of his Midwest victories. The electoral map in 2004 was almost exactly like the electoral map in 2000 except for three states that turned red, one of which was Iowa. In that state, three-fourths of registered voters voted, and one-third of those voting identified as evangelical—they voted for Bush seven to one.[45] Funny thing is, Bush won Iowa by less than 1 percent.

The perennial bellwether state of Ohio was one of the most competitive and hardly fought in 2004. Republicans significantly outorganized Democrats in Ohio, but the Kerry campaign still made attempts to target Ohio voters based on religion. One Ohio Democratic Party mailing featured a quote from John Kerry that said, "I believe that those of us guided by faith have to live out our faith . . . If you believe in the teachings of Jesus Christ, and I do, then you believe that you have some responsibility to other people."[46] In contrast to that Kerry mailing, an Ohio direct mailing went out that featured a church with a family and the caption "Protect Life, Strengthen Families, Defend Marriage" clearly in support of the conservative position.[47] Karl Rove made a specific effort to go after Ohio churches, so much so that the Bush campaign had ten church registration coordinators for Ohio alone.[48] Many Ohio clergy attended sessions on how to discuss the election from the pulpit in a legally safe way, the Southern Baptist Convention launched IvoteValues. com, and evangelical pastor Rick Warren sent a letter to 136,000 pastors asking them to consider candidate positions on a number of major social issues.[49] And the same-sex marriage amendment on the ballot in Ohio, which further rallied conservative Christian voters, passed with 67 percent of the vote.[50] Again, it is fully plausible that the increase in religiously motivated voters gave Bush his Ohio victory.

How Did It Happen?

So we know now that the 2004 presidential campaign represented a marked increase in the influence of religion on presidential campaigns. The prince that we had in office, George W. Bush, was allowed to stay there for four more years in large part due to concerns centered around religion. That, along with the ongoing Iraq and Afghanistan Wars and leftover fears of another terrorist attack, made for an election in which it was possible for religion to be a determining factor. Credit, though, must go to the Republican Party. They, led by Karl Rove, strategically utilized fear to appeal for the continuation of their leadership. They recognized that their 2000 popular vote loss was partially due to the lack of turnout by evangelical Christians, and they heightened the importance of wedge issues like gay marriage and abortion to drive the higher turnout that led to their win. The Democratic

Party tried, they made an effort, but Kerry couldn't overcome the perception that he was lacking in both substance and sincerity. As a result, the incumbent prince was reelected.

NOVEMBER 4, 2008

I grew up hearing adults talk about where they were when certain events occurred. Over the years I heard almost all of my older teachers recount their experiences learning of President Kennedy's and MLK's assassinations. My mom, who has never been very political, would tell her stories about other things that were particularly meaningful for her, like the Sixers winning the NBA Championship in 1983. These moments, whether major tragedy or celebrated accomplishment, seem to etch markers on the memory. As time goes on, all of us connect events to places, sounds, and even people with whom we experienced the events.

By the time November 2008 rolled around I had experienced such a moment at least once with September 11. A little over seven years before the night of the 2008 presidential election, I was just a thirteen-year-old eighth grader, who despite living in the complex world of middle school, lived within a somewhat simpler American political framework. As I sat there in my third-period social studies class at Tredyffrin/Easttown Middle School—I actually remember where my seat was in the room—our principal, Dr. Steve Riggs, came on the public address system and announced that two planes had hit the Twin Towers in New York. To this day, I'm not sure whether or not we saw the towers collapse live, but I distinctly remember watching them collapse on the classroom television. It took me (and my peers) a while to realize that what happened was an act of terrorism. That day the television in the classroom, then one of those bulky box TVs, was fixed on the news. In the days and weeks that followed, the entire outlook of the nation changed. I can also remember watching George W. Bush just a few days later in what has been recognized as a high point of his presidency. With a bullhorn raised to the mouth, Bush proclaimed, "I can hear you! The rest of the world hears you! And the people—and the people who knocked these buildings down will hear all of us soon."[1] I'm pretty sure I watched that moment live. That had to be the single greatest moment of George W. Bush's time in office. That moment at Ground Zero represented a president in the ultimate fulfillment of his role as prince.

Seven years later I was a junior at George Washington University (GWU) in DC. As a spoiler alert I'll admit that never in my life have I experienced something like election night '08. There simply are not words to describe the jubilation that possessed the entire District of Columbia. The type of spontaneous celebration that we were a part of that night was almost otherworldly. One sees images on television of countries where some revolution has occurred, and the masses gather in some open square to take down a colossal statue of the tyrannical dictator. That night there was no single open square, there was no tall statue, nor dictator, but there was a unique energy, and I'm not sure I've felt anything like that in the twelve years that have passed. The evening of the first election of Barack Obama meant something greater than the celebrations happening in the moment. It represented the feelings and spirit that many had about the reality of a black presidency.

Summer & Fall 2008

My memories of the period preceding the election are of an election season that was never ending. In the moment it felt like the campaign was dragging on forever, and indeed there was a long period between the beginning of the campaign and its conclusion. Some of the length of the campaign was a result of many people not giving Obama a chance initially. Regardless of what revisionists want to say, Hillary Clinton was the overwhelming favorite to win the Democratic primary well into the campaign, and many of both major parties' elite didn't expect Obama to win. I remember when former House majority leader Tom Delay visited GWU in the Fall of 2007, and I had the opportunity to ask him about Barack Obama. I raised my hand during question time and inquired about Delay's assessment of the junior senator from Illinois. Delay made it clear for the audience that he didn't think Obama had a chance. In fact, he said something like, "He doesn't have a chance." Delay suggested that if and when Obama really did start to rise, the powers that be would throw all of their resources into defeating him. Looking back on Delay's comments that evening, they are one part comical, but also one part indicative of the lack of respect Obama was given by many, including many in his own party.

In the Summer of '08, during the traditional national party convention season, the nation was treated to two vastly different images of party politics. On August 28 Obama took the stage in Denver, Colorado, to "with profound gratitude and great humility" accept the nomination for the presidency.[2] Even then, one got the sense that the individual speaking on the television was on the verge of making history, if for no other reason than he had already made history. There had never been another major party nominee who looked like Obama. He was already a first. The slogans about hope and change still meant something that August, and watching on television, you could feel that there were legitimate hope and certain change coming.

During his acceptance speech Obama painted a picture of a country with big problems. "We meet at one of those defining moments—

a moment when our nation is at war, our economy is in turmoil, and the American promise has been threatened once more."[3] Despite calling out the big problems that America was facing, Obama still revealed what was at the core of so many Americans' frustration in the fall of 2008: George W. Bush.

> But the record's clear: John McCain has voted with George Bush 90 percent of the time. Sen. McCain likes to talk about judgment, but really, what does it say about your judgment when you think George Bush has been right more than 90 percent of the time?[4]

George W. Bush was an unpopular president, and the election was a referendum on both George W. Bush and Republican leadership. The economic challenges were mounting, the Iraq quagmire continued, and an almost palpable sense of Bush fatigue lingered in the air. Now in death, Obama's opponent, Mr. McCain, looks more and more like the good man he was. I'm sure when history weighs national Republican figures in the balances, it's going to find many wanting and others like McCain looking like individuals ahead of their time. History will probably agree that McCain just ran for president at the wrong time. Obama wisely called out McCain's conservative voting record, despite his maverick tendencies, and made every attempt to remind voters of their dissatisfaction with the Republican president in office.

As happens every presidential election year, there was a second major political party convention, and Mr. McCain had his own opportunity to speak to the nation. The 2008 Republican National Convention was fraught with roadblocks and hurdles from the start. A major hurricane, Gustav, forced Republicans to cease most of the politicking on the first night of their gathering. Later that week, McCain and his running mate Sarah Palin accepted their party's nomination in the Twin Cities, likely knowing that they didn't have a good chance of winning. McCain began his acceptance speech, stating, "Tonight, I have a privilege given few Americans: the privilege of accepting our party's nomination for president of the United States."[5] McCain was right; few people ever stand in the position he stood in, which is part of what made Obama such a star. After 230-plus years, our nation was finally at the brink of having a person of color serve in its top leadership role. Maybe it was the recognition that Obama really was the frontrunner that led Mr. McCain to take a more conciliatory approach near the end of his acceptance speech.

> Finally, a word to Sen. Obama and his supporters. We'll go at it over the next two months. That's the nature of these contests, and there are big differences between us. But you have my respect and admiration. Despite our differences, much more unites us than divides us. We are fellow Americans, an association that means more to me than any other. We're dedicated to the proposition that all people are created equal and endowed by our Creator with inalienable rights. No country ever had a greater cause than that. And I wouldn't be an American worthy of the name if I didn't honor Sen. Obama and his supporters for their achievement.[6]

It didn't matter though, the conventions didn't really matter, and McCain's desperate attempt to woo voters with his choice of Sarah Palin didn't matter. By the fall the electorate was mostly sold on Obama. The last reputable poll that showed McCain leading was one from my own alma mater, GWU. The GWU/Battleground poll surveyed one thousand likely voters over a week in September, and McCain held a two-point edge. The last date on which McCain held the lead in the RealClearPolitics.com average was September 16. That day the RCP average showed McCain besting Obama 46.3 to 45 percent. The next day the RCP average had both candidates tied, and the polls showed McCain trailing Obama for the rest of the campaign.[7]

For politics junkies and political science majors like myself, all indications were that America was about to do something historic in a matter of weeks. Although we held cautious optimism, we knew that this presidential election was going to be different. For me, it was the first time I was able to cast a vote for president. It was a little anticlimactic that I had to do it via absentee ballot, but a thrill nonetheless. Here I was, having grown up being told I could be the first black president, casting my first presidential vote for the first black president. I always found that suggestion to be amusing because as much as I am a student of politics, I have never wanted to be president. Sure, I had voted in midterm elections, but 2008 was the first time I would get to help decide the leader of the country. We knew that Obama was going to win, but we didn't know how he was going to win, and we probably couldn't have predicted the spontaneous celebration that would ensue.

Election Night

The Friday before Election Day, October 31, was both Halloween and the day of the Phillies World Series Parade. I have no idea how the rest of the country felt, but it was historic for those of us from the Philadelphia region. Philly was euphoric from the suburbs to the city. Me and some of my college friends from the Philly area drove up the morning of the parade and managed to get down to the sports complex in South Philly by car. Since most people took public transportation to the parade (which turned out to be a mess), those of us who drove to the stadiums ended up getting to enjoy the parade the most. I'm recounting these memories to express just how much of a celebratory season it already was in my life, and I'm willing to admit that I'm biased because of it. I see the beginning of November 2008 through rose-colored glasses. That fall, at least for me, was a season of winning. My team won the World Series, and my candidate won the presidency. Phrases like "from the White House to the Night House" were commonplace among black people at that time. There was a sense of pride not just in black America but among young progressives in general. The parade was Friday, and the election was Tuesday. The spirit of the times was memorialized through the words of hip-hop moguls like Jay-Z and Sean Combs. The former was recorded as saying, "Rosa sat so Martin could walk; Martin walked so Obama could run; Obama is running so we all can fly!"[8] Combs said, "I felt the whole civil rights movement, I felt all that energy, and I felt my kids. It was all there at one time. It was a joyous moment."[9] Both rappers were but two of the myriad celebrities whose words help tell the story of the season's significance.

On election night many of us were gathered in a townhouse on Twenty-Third Street, and the TV in the common area was set to election night coverage on CNN. The energy was building, and finally at 11:00 p.m. Eastern time as polls in California, Hawaii, Idaho, Oregon, and Washington closed, Wolf Blitzer made the announcement, "CNN can now project that Barack Obama, forty-seven years old, will become the president-elect of the United States."[10] The rest of the night became a little bit of a blur, but in the midst of the yelling, we could hear Blitzer quickly follow up the announcement with, "And now, he will be the first African American president of the United States."

Perhaps my memories are best expressed by my own words back in 2008. In the wee hours of the morning, after returning home from traveling around DC celebrating—and I do mean traveling, we left the White House and somehow ended up on U-Street—I opened my computer and typed a letter to the editor that appeared in the November 6, 2008, edition of GWU's newspaper, the *Hatchet*.

> Several hours ago, after hearing the results of the 2008 presidential election, several friends and I proceeded to run to the White House, darting past Thurston on the way and picking up tens of accompanying students. We were lucky enough to be a part of the initial group of students to gather out front, but that did not stop us from staying long enough to be joined by hundreds and perhaps thousands of GW— and eventually DC-area—students . . . While I will always consider the election of the first black president an incredibly significant moment in our nation's history and indeed my life, even more meaningful will be that moment in which GW students and staff came together and gathered at the center of American democracy—excited, energized, but most importantly, unified.[11]

Other newspapers and media outlets also covered the spontaneous gathering at the White House. Reporters for CNN wrote, "At least one thousand people gathered on Washington's Pennsylvania Avenue in front of the White House late Tuesday night, shouting 'Obama! Obama!' and 'Yes we Can!' Uniformed Secret Service officers were overheard saying they'd never seen anything like it."[12] There are a lot of moments of spontaneous agitation, but there aren't too many moments of spontaneous celebration. When they happen, they should be treasured. I don't know that I'll ever experience anything like it again. What I do remember is the feeling, and the feeling was that the right prince was about to take the leadership of the country. Apparently, that feeling wasn't restricted to the District of Columbia. There are other stories about similar celebrations in cities across the country, but there was one official celebration, and that was the one at

Grant Park in Chicago. Princeton's Keeanga-Yamahtta Taylor wrote,

> The excitement about Obama turned into postelection euphoria. That was certainly the feeling in Chicago on election night, when a cross section of the city converged in Grant Park to hear the country's first black president-elect address the nation. It was a rare, almost strange scene to see a multiracial crowd gathered in Chicago, one of the most segregated cities in the United States. That was the power of Obama's calls for hope and change.[13]

For those of us who grew up in the '90s with Nickelodeon, Discmans, and America in peacetime, the beginning of the 2000s was a little depressing. Economic challenge, major natural disasters, wars and rumors of wars . . . On November 4, 2008, for a change, hope was on the horizon, and in the fall of 2008, hope was exactly what the country needed.

HOPE AND FEAR

hen we look at the roles of prince, priest, and prophet, each of them in their own way is supposed to be an instrument of hope, but ultimately the prince is supposed to inspire the hope of the nation. In the Old Testament, Saul was initially seen as an instrument of hope. The idea was that he, as the new human prince, could go before the Israelites and defend them against their foes. He was supposed to be the one who would lead them out into the battles against groups like the Philistines and bring about their protection and security—at least that was the idea. According to the biblical account, some of those things happened initially, but they were not sustained in the long run. Eventually, Saul's personal leadership flaws got the best of him. Saul is a great example of how unconquered fears in a leader will inhibit their ability to be an instrument of hope. Sure, we all have fears, but when our fears, like Saul's, are unmanaged, they prevent hope from rising. Every so often, when we examine the shortcomings of leaders, particularly those who occupy the role of prince, we find that those shortcomings are manifestations of fears. For obvious reasons, decision-makers who serve a princely function are particularly susceptible to the fear of doing the wrong thing, either tactically or verbally.

As we continue to look at the formations of the Obama presidency, I suspect that some conservatives would take my use of the word *prince* to be support for the idea that Barack Obama's presidency existed within some sort of imperial framework. I have never understood how

Barack Obama was viewed as imperial, but that suspicion is worth addressing. Many conservatives were never going to view President Obama as legitimate, no matter what he said or did. Facing the onslaught of conspiracy theories and quite frankly, racism, Obama was fighting the invisible winds of prejudice from the moment he was announced as the winner of the election. The current president is reaping the same fruit of conspiracy theories and lack of honor in large part because he was among the leaders of the movement to delegitimize his predecessor.

The Narrative of Hope

On January 20, 2009, well over one million people gathered on the National Mall to hear President Obama deliver his inaugural address. That morning started early for me, as I was one of the students invited to ride in the trolley that pulled GWU's inaugural float. The only reason I was invited was because I was serving as vice president of the student body. The float itself was tacky and ugly, but, hey, the university was represented, and we rode in the inaugural parade past the reviewing stand, so I should probably be grateful for the experience. Definitely a privilege, but also definitely anticlimactic. It would've been nice to be out on the mall with some of my other friends, not riding past it. Looking out in the trolley that pulled the float, we could see the hundreds of thousands of people on the mall. It was a sight to behold for sure. We were also able to hear the festivities live on the radio in the trolley, so all was not lost.

I have to admit, though, as one who was initially attracted to President Obama in large part because of his powerful ability to communicate (verbally and via pen), I wasn't really impressed with his first inaugural address. Some years of reflection have reminded me that inaugural addresses are really about history. They're also an opportunity to turn from the campaign to the work of uniting the country, and Obama really was a campaigner. Similar to his remarks at the convention several months before, Obama used his first inaugural address to acknowledge some of the difficulties facing the nation.

During the speech he stated,

> That we are in the midst of crisis is now well understood. Our nation is at war against a far-reaching network of violence and hatred. Our economy is badly weakened, a consequence of greed and irresponsibility on the part of some, but also our collective failure to make hard choices and prepare the nation for a new age. Homes have been lost, jobs shed, businesses shuttered. Our health care is too costly, our schools fail too many—and each day brings further evidence that the ways we use energy strengthen our adversaries and threaten our planet. These are the indicators of crisis, subject to data and statistics.[1]

Taken out of context that might be one of the most pessimistic paragraphs anyone will hear a president read. But of course, that paragraph was just one in a speech with many. Overall the speech was not pessimistic; it was in line with the theme of hope that had carried Obama to electoral victory. The new president mentioned *hope* three times in his first inaugural address; he mentioned *fear* twice. Knowing the little bit that I know about political messaging, I refuse to believe that the language choice was unintentional. The symbolism is powerful. "On this day, we gather because we have chosen *hope* over *fear*, unity of purpose over conflict and discord."[2]

A prince is setting the entire nation up for failure if he peddles fear. Looking at the historical rankings of American presidents, the most popular ones seem to be the ones that do the most to assuage fears. In the 2017 C-SPAN Presidential Historian Survey, Abraham Lincoln was ranked first on the list of the greatest American presidents. Historically Lincoln has been favored in such surveys because among other accomplishments, he fought against the fear of a divided country. The historical record is now full of examples of how Lincoln really did make good decisions that helped preserve our country even while the nation was on the brink of a permanent split. Franklin Roosevelt is listed at number three, and many Americans can quote his most famous line, "The only thing we have to fear is fear itself."[3] Roosevelt fought against the fear of depression and economic uncertainty. He made tough decisions that helped alleviate fears, which in turn helped restore some confidence to an economically depressed nation. How can we leave out George Washington? Second on the 2017 rankings list was the father of our country.[4] It was Washington, the charismatic Revolutionary War general and face of the one-dollar bill, who helped shape and lead a brand-new country. Fears are natural with anything new, as new things by default bring unknowns and ambiguity. It was in the face of these unknowns that General Washington used his charisma and stature to lead a new republic, establishing a precedent that largely still stands. In his first address as president of the United States, Obama called out the fears that were partially responsible for his election. "Less measurable, but no less profound, is a sapping of confidence across our land; a nagging *fear* that America's decline is inevitable, that the next generation must lower its sights."

It's no surprise that President Obama opted to reference words used by George Washington in his inaugural address. "Let it be told to the future world . . . that in the depth of winter, when nothing but *hope* and virtue could survive . . . that the city and the country, alarmed at one common danger, came forth to meet [it]." It turns out that George Washington didn't even compose those words. Washington asked that the words (penned by Thomas Paine) be read to his troops, almost like an eighteenth-century pregame speech from a coach. It stands to reason that raising hope isn't always about coming up with the right words; often it's about finding the right words and invoking them.

The new president followed up his Washingtonian quote with his third and final reference to hope. He stated, "With hope and virtue, let us brave once more the icy currents and endure what storms may come." The comedy is that every president faces icy currents and storms; it is part of the job. Again, our prince is elected. We almost had a female succeed Obama, but when we finally do have a female president, she too will be elected. Everyone running for that position makes promises, many of which they will not be able to keep. For that reason, so much of their success hinges on the attitude they're able to inspire. So much of how history judges them relates to the emotions they stir, and when history looks back on Obama it will have to at least acknowledge that he called the nation to hope. It helped that he looked like hope—an African American male ascending to the highest levels of political leadership in a country that was built on the subjugation of such individuals. It helped that he had a whole bestselling book about the audacity of hope. It helped that thematically, Obama constructed an argument for his leadership on the notion of using hope to advance the country. My better judgment tells me that over time history and the historians studying it will appreciate the narrative of hope, especially in light of the forces working against it.

Strategic Delegitimization

Who would've thought that just eight years to the day after the first African American president was sworn into office, Donald J. Trump would take the same oath on the same spot, facing the same mall, to lead the same country? Trump was the same man who had spent several years serving as the de facto voice for the birther movement. Birtherism promoted the idea that President Obama was not born in United States. Trump had the money and the platform and was the most notable individual to promote the conspiracy theory. One of my undergraduate professors, John Sides, joined several other political scientists in calling Trump "a virtual spokesperson for the 'birther' movement."[5]

When history looks back on this period, it's not going to look kindly on America's decision-making. In a democracy, elections, absent any cheating or rigging, expose the heart of a people. Polls can reveal some of that information as well. One of the most damning stains on the last ten years will be the data on just how many people questioned the legitimacy of the first black president.

The rumors about Obama's birth began in 2004 when an Illinois foe of then state senator Obama Andy Martin suggested Obama was a closet Muslim.[6] A rumor can be a powerful thing, especially when the kernel of truth is such that it can't be easily placed in the proper context. In 2004 the rumors weren't taken as seriously, because there was no real reason to invest the time and energy into examining them. Obama was only running for the United States Senate, and senators don't have to be born in the US. Also, everyone knew that the man circulating the rumors was a clear political enemy.

By April 2008 Obama was much more of a political force, and he was in a position to actually be the Democratic presidential nominee. At that point he was a legitimate threat to the established order, and those who had taken his political rise for granted understood that only more sinister tactics would be able to halt the Obama train. That month, an anonymous email was sent by Clinton supporters claiming that Obama was not born in Hawaii.[7] The rumor was picked up by others, and today we can say that the real originators of birtherism, at least in its more powerful form, were people in Obama's own party. Even though Obama went on to win the election, the rumors persisted, and two years into his presidency he was still dealing with the challenge of those who wanted to question whether or not he was a legitimate American citizen. An April 2011 poll showed that almost half of GOP voters believed Obama was not born in the US.[8] It's still amazing to me that after Obama was finally able to put the crazy rumors to rest, the country nevertheless elected the leading proponent of the dispelled rumors.

It's hard to say whether or not Trump was taken more seriously prior to becoming president than he is now. I remember the media buying into the Trump hype when the idea of him actually winning was laughable. Whether or not he was taken seriously before becoming president, Trump had a platform, and eventually his crazy birther ideas came to a head. As one reflects on the story arc of the birther drama, there was almost creepy foreshadowing happening in April 2011 when President Obama and his future successor came face-to-face at the Annual White House Correspondent's Dinner. This dinner is considered DC's version of the Oscars. Many Hollywood personalities attend, and the various media outlets that cover the White House do their best to get high-profile individuals at their tables. It's not unusual on the night of the event to see #nerdprom trending on Twitter, because that's really what the event is, a sort of prom for political nerds.

Just that week President Obama had finally released the longform version of his 1961 Hawaii birth certificate, an action that was supposed to offer definitive evidence that he was born in the United States. Many normal Americans accepted the proof, but of course Mr. Trump was in the audience with his doubts—or at least committed to promoting his doubts. During the dinner Obama spent several minutes during his monologue effectively taking a birther victory lap. Obama highlighted the foolishness of Mr. Trump's quest to prove he was not a citizen. At one point Obama said, "Say what you will about Mr. Trump, he certainly would bring some change to the White House. Let's see what we've got up there." And laughter arose as the screens behind President Obama showed a satirical "Trump White House Resort and Casino." It's likely that no one in the room knew that in less than six years Mr. Trump would actually be bringing change to the White House as the elected president.[9]

Contrast Trump's actions on birtherism with John McCain's. On October 10, 2008, John McCain held a campaign event where a woman stated, "I gotta ask you a question, I do not, ah, believe in, I can't trust Obama. I, I have read about him and he's not, he's not, he's a, um, he's an Arab." It's important that the lady's "ums" and "ahs" be included to really understand the stupidity of the question/statement. Unlike so many other Republicans who didn't have the testicular fortitude to do the same, McCain plainly shot down the woman's suggestion that Obama was not American with words that received a lot of airplay when McCain passed away in the fall of 2018. "No ma'am," McCain said. "He's a decent family man, a citizen that I just happen to have disagreements with on fundamental issues, and that's what this campaign is all about."[10]

The rumors about Obama's nativity persisted much longer than they should have. A YouGov poll from 2016 found that 53 percent of Republicans didn't believe that Obama was born in the US.[11] Quite frankly, given the evidence that was presented to the contrary, that's pitiful. It's a sad statistic and even worse commentary on lingering bigotry in our country. That so many people couldn't see this brown man as the legitimate leader he was is evidence of the power of the racism that persists in our nation. It is also evidence of the power of fear, fear of the other, fear of those who don't look like the norm, and fear of the ascendance of an entire marginalized group of people.

The Narrative of Fear

The narrative of fear is what carried Trump to the White House. The example of the previous Republican presidential candidate is of one who put integrity and character above political expedience. As a result, now in death, most of us view John McCain as one who can be respected, regardless of how many votes he cast that we disagreed with. One is left wondering what will be said about Mr. Trump at his funeral. A legacy, of course, is about more than what a president does while he or she is in office. It's also about the decisions they made and the things they said on their path to the White House. On his way to the White House, Mr. Trump tread through the mud of prejudice and racist innuendo. His path was one that included wading through murky waters of xenophobia and unbridled misogyny. Our country has never seen anything like Mr. Trump in the highest office, in large part because previous presidents, for better or for worse, have called our nation to reject fear. In direct opposition to what those forty-three other men understood, Trump has instead called our nation to embrace fear. If Mr. Obama's selection called to mind the selection of Saul, his presidency was the opposite. For all of his flaws, Mr. Obama led with integrity. Mr. Trump, on the other hand, is likely to be remembered like Saul, one who's erratic behavior and lack of integrity brought about his downfall.

Many preachers will tell you fear is the opposite of faith, and although they are not in the position of priest, the prince has a role to play in pointing people in the direction of faith. In the grand scheme of civil religion, a successful prince understands the need to be a civil

spiritual leader. That's why we look to the president for not only political action, but words of comfort when catastrophic things happen.
Just like the Old Testament princes who, although not priests, had
much to say about faith in the lands they presided over, so does the
American prince have a lot to do with the extent to which faith or fear
is elevated at a given moment.

Make no mistake, *civil religion* is a real thing, and one that I didn't
make up. In their well-known book, *Religion and Politics in the United
States*, now in its eighth edition, Kenneth Wald and Allison Calhoun-
Brown describe civil religion as the "constant recourse to religious images and symbols in American political culture." They go on to say
that "by imparting a sacred character to the nation, civil religion enables people of diverse faiths to harmonize their religious and political
beliefs."[12] When one takes a more exhaustive look at civil religion in
the United States, they find that much of it is about promoting faith.
By faith, I don't mean belief in a particular religion, but faith in the
hope sort of sense. Along those lines, Hebrews is the book of the Bible
that probably does the best job of defining faith. "Now faith is the substance of things hoped for, the evidence of things not seen."[13] Faith
and hope are inextricably tied together, maybe not the same thing, but
the latter indicates that the former is present.

Our governmental leaders have not just a role but a major role to
play in ministering to people. Previously this played out every time a
national tragedy occurred and the president stood in some hallowed
space to offer words of comfort. These events were *previously* understood to be an absolute part of the job of the prince. Not so much
anymore. We're now in an age when communities ask the current
president to stay away from the scene of tragedy, just because his presence is so divisive. That's what fear does; it eventually weakens the one
who peddles it.

The contrast between the fearmongering of this president and the hope narrative that defined the Obama campaign is stark. Princes are selected for reasons and also deposed for reasons. Mr. Obama was elected because the electorate embraced his idea of hope, and Mr. Trump was elected because he tapped into a powerful vein of fear.

One image that will forever be a representation of the election of 2008 is Shepard Fairey's Obama HOPE poster. Inspired by images of President John F. Kennedy and Abraham Lincoln, Fairey created an image that was seemingly everywhere. The poster helped iconize Obama and may have aided in producing the magnitude of his electoral victory. Imprinted in big bold font on the poster is the word HOPE. Hope was what Mr. Obama was seeking to bring to the nation, and in some ways, he was initially successful. For a period of time, measured differently according to how much one likes Mr. Obama, the new president was able to be a physical representation of some progress in America. I never thought as a kid in the 1990s that our nation would see a black president as soon as it did. That we had one standing in front of us was amazing.

If we say then that 2008 was all about hope, we have to say that 2016, like 2004, was all about fear. Sure, the prevailing slogan in 2016 was "Make America Great Again," but the word *again* said more than five letters suggested. To many of us, "Make America Great Again" was code for "America Is Not What It Once Was" and "I Can Help Prevent America from Becoming What It's about to Be." Both ideas speak to fears and are the direct opposite of the hope that calls a people to not just the best in terms of economic productivity, but the best in terms of values. Riding a wave of hope, Obama was swept into office in 2008 only for him and the country to find out that hope and high expectations can be a toxic mix if mishandled. The biblical account shows that the Israelites learned this lesson with Saul.

THE RESOLUTE DESK

U pon taking office, every leader is met with expectations, both of them as individuals and of whatever office they hold. For the president of the United States, the Oval Office is the traditional seat of authority, even though many recent presidents have chosen to use other rooms in the White House as their primary workspace. No matter where the president may speak, the Oval Office remains the most powerful symbol of the executive position in our government. Regardless of the specific desk the president chooses to place in the Oval Office, the room and the decisions made at that desk have enormous consequences in the face of even greater expectations. Any conversation about the expectations we have of our prince equivalent goes well beyond a physical office. The conversation has to include the overall social contract that We the People have with our government, the focal point of which is the president. We need to be reminded that our presidents are not invincible, yet we also need to know that they're not really rational actors either. Like everyone in public policy, presidents are constrained by the effects of their humanity. Like the forty-two men who preceded him, Barack Obama fit this mold of leadership: vulnerable, constrained, and ultimately human.

Expectations of Princes

No matter what form a government takes, whether autocracy, oligarchy, or democracy, there is always some entity that takes on the role of prince. Although not all of them used the exact language, the who's who list of Western political theorists wrote about the *social contract* from which the authority of government executives was derived. In addition to Locke and Hobbes, Hugo Grotius, Samuel von Pufendorf, Jean-Jacques Rousseau, and Immanuel Kant are among those who described such a social contract and what they believed it meant for leadership.

A contract is supposed to be a means of bringing about predictability and stability. The same principle was at play in the Old Testament with the law. The idea was that if one party did a particular thing, another party promised to do another. Even today, when two or more parties enter into a contract, they do so seeking assurances.

No matter who the prince is, there has to be a recognition that the prince can't do everything, and at some point, the prince will be limited by their own capacity. In his book *Crash the Chatterbox*, pastor Steven Furtick wrote, "Disappointment is the gap between what I expect and what I experience."[1] The problem for us is our expectations of leaders. Simply put, we expect too much of our leaders. The Obama presidency, for all of its successes, was also characterized by a tremendous amount of disappointment. It was a presidency that exemplified Furtick's description. In some corners the expectation was that this knight in melanin armor would come in and right all of America's racial wrongs. In other corners the expectation was that the same knight would valiantly (and easily) deliver universal healthcare, especially given the fact that his own party controlled the legislative branch during his first two years in office. Of course, history records that things didn't play out that way. The gap that remained left many with a sense of disappointment.

The academic discipline of public administration has analyzed some of the things that go into the policy making that presidents are supposed to lead. Herbert Simon famously examined the limitations of leaders, and the crux of Simon's theory was that those making public policy weren't completely rational actors because they were limited by various constraints.[2] By itself, that theory shouldn't strike one as too controversial, because as humans we all have limits, or as Simon called them, constraints. These constraints make it impossible for those in public policy, like a president, to act in complete rationality. Simon laid out three reasons why this was the case.

The first reason was that no one could possibly have complete knowledge of all the many consequences of their choices. When a president makes a decision, whether it's a military decision, an economic decision, or an administrative one, they are acting in a vacuum of knowledge. Sure, they may receive advice, but there is no possible way they can know all of the many consequences of a given action. Second, Simon suggested that people needed to use imagination to attach a value to each of the possible consequences of a decision, because consequences are things of the future and they only arise after a choice has been made. Third, complete rationality would imply that one had total knowledge of all possible alternatives when people almost never know about all of the possible alternatives.[3] The summary of the theory is that public policy actors make decisions with the best information they have, but don't necessarily make rational ones.

Many of those who are most critical of the Obama presidency cite actions like expanding America's drone program and the increase in the deportation of undocumented individuals as among the policy areas in which Obama did not meet their expectations. I was stunned a few years ago to learn that Byrne Grants, those enabling local law enforcement agencies to purchase military-grade materials, increased at Obama's direction. In her dense and prophetic work, *The New Jim Crow*, Michelle Alexander detailed how Obama's Economic Recovery

Act of 2009 "included more than $2 billion in new Byrne funding and an additional $600 million to increase state and local law enforcement across the country."[4] While many Obama supporters like myself cried, "black lives matter!" and decried the use of military artillery against poor black individuals, the truth of Obama's indirect support of such foolishness remained.

Some of those consequences that presidents don't have total knowledge about involve the way people perceive their decisions. There were certainly moments when one had to wonder if President Obama was fully aware of how people on the ground felt about his presidency. I always felt like he was doing a good job, but I was biased. I was in my DC undergraduate bubble during the first few years of the Obama presidency, and I was in my Ivy League graduate school bubble during the later years. As time passed it dawned on me that not all black people were enamored with the Obama presidency. In the words of Michael Eric Dyson, "black America beamed with pride when Obama became the most powerful black man in history. Many black folk believed that Obama's victory was their triumph."[5]

I have to take a minute to acknowledge the media problem. By that I mean the fact that the mainstream media has an undue amount of influence on our choices. To see evidence of what I'm talking about, one need only think about the attention the mainstream media gave Mr. Trump. The media hyped his campaign so much until the Frankenstein they created was elected president. The media also hyped Obama and set many Americans up for letdowns in certain areas, like race relations. The media put forth an image of Obama's win as a "beacon of post-racial America" which critical observers probably recognized from the beginning as a false image.[6] How could America possibly become post-racial when race and racism were etched into the fabric of every facet of it? Race is a social construction, but it doesn't just go away when a black man, even if he is a biracial one, suddenly becomes president of the United States. What the media was really suggesting was that if a black man became president, maybe racism was about to go away, or maybe race didn't matter anymore. Even most black kids can articulate the silliness in those ideas. To borrow words from the title of one of Cornel West's most famous works, race matters, and the expectation that it would matter less because of Obama was an ignorant one. If anything, the Obama presidency caused race to matter more.

The Power of a Desk

I've already noted that each generation has its own concept of what is and what isn't presidential. There was obviously a time when social media wasn't a thing, and I'm old enough to remember that time. There was a time when we didn't expect our presidents to tweet out messages, because Twitter wasn't around. I think it has been amazing to see how social media has transformed the ways in which all of us communicate. Things like trending topics and viral videos have fundamentally changed our politics. It's probably safe to say that the Obama campaign had fully mastered social media, but the Obama administration never fully mastered the Oval Office address. I believe some of that failure had to do with the avoidance of the Resolute Desk. That is to say, the record shows that President Obama had no aversion to speeches, but certainly had one to delivering speeches seated at the Resolute Desk.

On June 15, 2010 as a massive oil crisis was happening in the Gulf of Mexico, President Obama delivered his first major address from the Oval Office. That day, a year and a half into his presidency, the president, seated and presidentially postured, made every attempt to display leadership. He did so even as one of the worst environmental crises in America's history was unfolding off our southern shore. Obama was sitting behind the Resolute Desk, that big oak gift delivered by Queen Victoria to president Rutherford B. Hayes almost a century and a half ago. The desk is the same wooden antique that John F. Kennedy Jr. played under in a photo that has since become famous. Twice, President Obama sat at that desk and spoke to the nation as its leader. The second occasion was August 31 of the same year, when President Obama announced the end of combat missions in Iraq.

Obama's third Oval Office address, unlike the first two, was delivered standing behind a lectern. The optics probably didn't work out the way the president had hoped. On this occasion, December 6, 2015, President Obama addressed the horrific mass shooting in San Bernardino, California, in which sixteen individuals lost their lives and twenty-four were injured.

As refined and polished as the Obama administration's press arm attempted to be, at times President Obama failed to master the optics of the office. Evidence of this is found in his poll numbers. At the end of May 2013, Obama's approval ratings began to fall underwater, and it's likely that the government shutdown of that year was responsible. The calendar year October 2013 through October 2014 was the worst for Obama as far as approval ratings were concerned. During these months Obama's unpopularity peaked at 56 percent.[7] Despite having won re-election, people were waxing disappointed in his leadership. In the same span of time the unrest in Ferguson, Missouri, served as but one additional event that highlighted some of the reasons why the president was so unpopular. By December of the following year, close to the time Obama had restored full diplomatic relations with Cuba, his approval rating had rebounded significantly.

The title of an NPR article from December 2014 expresses the reality of that time: "Obama Finds Reset Button with 2 Years to Go: Is It Too Late?"[8] Of course it wasn't too late, and there were definitely several good things that happened over the course of Obama's remaining two years in office, but there were times when Obama made things more difficult on himself. I'm speaking of the times when Americans needed a sermon or pep talk, and instead were treated to measured lectures. This was the case with the civil unrest that consumed Ferguson, Missouri, in November 2014. Even as cars were burning and Ferguson was in an uproar, a split screen showed the burning buildings on one side and a cool, calm, and collected president on the other. Referring to the horrible optics of that moment, a *Washington Post* article said, "Commanders-in-chief are not the ones directing news broadcasts. They can control what they say—they can't control the optics."[9] Recognizing that they can't control the optics, it's incumbent upon a president to consider the optics, even as they consider their words.

That's why I continue to lament the lack of Oval Office speeches from Obama. Even more, I lament the lack of Oval Office speeches delivered from behind the Resolute Desk. Maybe I'm just one of the many who is simply married to the image of the presidents that came immediately before Obama. Maybe I have some sort of soul tie to the images of George H. W. Bush, Bill Clinton, and George W. Bush sitting at a desk in the Oval Office and using the words, "My fellow Americans . . ." to launch well-worded rhetorical presentations. Maybe. Or maybe I'm one of many Americans who had a concept of what was presidential in our minds and yearned to see Obama replicate that at critical times. No, I'm not suggesting that he wasn't presidential or didn't conduct himself in a presidential way. I'm saying that there were moments when President Obama did not make full use of the tools at his disposal. The Resolute Desk was one such tool that was not utilized the way it should've been. It's possible that had President Obama delivered more speeches in crisis from the Resolute Desk in the Oval Office, it may—emphasis on may—have helped him connect more with those who didn't fully trust him. I know some will feel that is an unfair assertion, but it's worth further examination as the post Obama years grow longer.

Nevertheless, as I've already acknowledged, I understand that there were many people who were never going to trust President Obama—some because of his liberal history, some because of his lack of tenure in the federal government, many because he was black. Regardless, the Resolute Desk speaks to the expectations that once defined the presidency. For many years Americans expected the president to communicate major messages from the Oval Office, seated at the particular desk that was in the office at that time. Not so much anymore. Expectations are one of the things that have been most negatively affected by the Trump presidency. One is left wondering what Americans' expectations of a president are now. Does the current presidency mean that all future presidents will be able to tweet what they want no matter how vulgar or childish? Will all future presidents be able to deliver major messages in any format they wish, be it impulsive social media post or meme? None of us can say for sure. What we can be certain of is the high impact of expectations when it comes to the office of president and how one's work in that position is received.

Part II
The Priests

STRANGE FIRE

Virtually every culture has at least one form of religion or evidence of spirituality. Normally there are intermediaries, or priests, to help carry out the ritual of the religion. In America, religion and the institutions that sustain it have been at the core of our ups and downs for over 230 years. We sometimes downplay the role of religion in our country's history even though most of the men and women who originally colonized America came to the new world seeking religious freedom. Despite what some may say, the church still plays a central role in our country. The priesthood, the church, or what I like to call the *American religious complex* is still important, and today it displays a critical dichotomy between one version of American religion and the other, largely broken down along racial lines. In a sermon in 1986, the late right reverend Ozro Thurston Jones Jr., a Philadelphia theologian and leading bishop in the Church of God in Christ, described how interesting it was that a majority of African Americans were Christian given that the version of Christianity they received from white slaveowners was a religion that the slave owners themselves were not practicing.[1] I liken this to the *strange fire* of which we read about in the Old Testament.

There is an account in the 10th chapter of Leviticus that speaks to the plight of religion in the United States. So much of the hypocritical rhetoric that rises from parts of our country is steeped in religious language and a fake attempt at morality. It is the byproduct of a biblical zeal that justifies violence. Robert Jewett suggests that this zeal "contends that righteous violence can redeem other people, demonstrate one's superiority over rival forces, and even convert the world" and "justifies the most appalling atrocities believing that violence is necessary to produce and keep peace."[2] When one peels back the layers of inconsistency, they see just how much the rhetoric doesn't match the Bible that many faith leaders claim to base their beliefs on. If there was a match, there wouldn't be such a persistent tolerance of systemic racism in parts of American Christianity. Above all else, priests perform religious rites and facilitate worship. In 2019, one is left questioning just what is being worshipped by large swaths of the American priesthood. Is money being worshipped? Is white Christian nationalism being worshipped? Is the president of the United States being worshipped? In various places, the answer to all three of these questions is yes.

The Leviticus Account

The Pentateuch, which consists of the first five books of the Bible, is full of history, but within the law-focused book of Leviticus, there are only a few historical narratives. For me, the most intriguing of those narratives has always been the account of the *strange fire* that killed two men named Nadab and Abihu.[3] These two men were the sons of Aaron, the brother of Moses. The text reinforces a primary theme of the Old Testament, that a holy God requires holiness. That was part of the contract: the people live holy, and a holy God protects them. At its core, the story of the immediate deaths of these two priests emphasizes the holiness—adherence to God's specified methods and practices—that God required of those who were commissioned to serve him.

It is impossible to fully contextualize the deaths of Nadab and Abihu without some background knowledge on the priestly order of which they were a part. Both were sons of Aaron, Moses's brother, and together with their father, they and their two other brothers were set apart by God to serve as priests. The Exodus story details how, after delivering the Israelites from Egyptian captivity, God allowed Moses to be their prophetic leader and guide. Moses's participation was significant because it was to him that God gave the famous Ten Commandments and established an agreement with the Israelites. On the face of things, the agreement was a simple one, and the simplicity was that if Moses and the Israelites did as God had commanded and followed the law, they would remain successful. The agreement extended to specific offices, including the office of priest. Unfortunately, the two priests in this story did not stick to the agreement, and their deaths in the 10th chapter of Leviticus highlighted the severity of the punishments when commissioned priests deviated from the rules. A more specific part of the agreement that appears earlier in the Old Testament is that Aaron and all of his sons were to be set apart to serve as priests. It was theirs to facilitate the process of worship for the nation of Israel. To be set apart for such a high and holy function was an honor no doubt, but it was also a tremendous responsibility.

I may be partial, but I still believe that the priesthood is a special vocation. I'm not solely speaking about priesthood in the Catholic sense, where one has to remain celibate and generally only wears clerical attire. I'm speaking about the overall call to work in the area of faith. One biblical commentary states, "The primary idea of a priest is that of a man who performs some function on behalf of men toward God which would not be equally acceptable by God if performed by themselves . . ."[4] The Old Testament priesthood, like many other modern professions, required a certification process, and the primary requirement for certification was God's anointing, or his power. I sometimes think we would do well to view more of our life's work in that context. Those of us in various forms of Christian ministry often talk about our work in terms of being *called* to do what we do, but I think such a view should be extended to all of life. It's not that everything should be in religious vocabularies, but that we should see life as an opportunity to fulfill our calling, whatever that may be.

At this point in the Old Testament the priesthood was only open to certain individuals from one family line. Yet despite the exclusivity and particularity of their vocation, the priests, as *The Pulpit Commentary* describes, were serving *on behalf of* the community. Their status as workers on behalf of others implied responsibility, and in the 1st verse of chapter 10, Nadab and Abihu were seemingly carrying out their priestly duties. It was only their deaths that exposed for future readers the brothers' failure to carry out their priestly duties with fidelity.

As priests, these men were not only set apart, but they were uniquely *anointed* for the job. The actual act of anointing involved someone else performing the ritual of pouring oil upon the heads of the individuals who were to serve. The 8th chapter of Leviticus records how Moses, following God's instructions, "took some of the anointing oil . . . and sprinkled it upon Aaron and his garments, and also upon his sons and his sons' garments."[5] With that act, Moses set Aaron and his sons apart from the rest of Israel for the special duty of facilitating the worship of their God. In many ways, the act symbolically demonstrated that God's power and ability were with them. But as the modern axiom states,

"With much power comes much responsibility."

The point is, there were requirements and restrictions placed upon those who were called to do God's special work. The Bible seems replete with examples of God placing restrictions on those who have been anointed for special services and the added responsibilities thrust upon them. God gave strict orders about how Aaron and his sons were to dress, when they were supposed to work, and what they were supposed to eat. They were supposed to be *holy*.[6]

Another book of the Pentateuch, Exodus, details God's instructions to Moses to make Aaron and his sons special garments to wear. The full ensemble included ornate robes or *ephods*, special belts, and even special head coverings. It is clear that everything the priests publicly wore and did was to be accompanied by a sense of dignity, and that was to ultimately glorify God. Presumably, failure to glorify God would result in punishments like that which was given to Nadab and Abihu.

Even beyond the physical dignity that the job required, the priesthood also required spiritual dignity. God had instructed Moses to make for the priestly order linen undergarments that were supposed to cover them from the waist to the thigh.[7] The priests were to always have on these undergarments whenever they approached God, or else they would die. The exegete in me gets excited when I study this because there is so much symbolism here. It is apparent from the instructions of Exodus that not only did God require the cleanliness and appropriate appearance of the priestly order on the outside, but also God expected the same of those parts which could not be seen—the nature of their office required it. Consider that in terms of the modern American priesthood. Not only is there supposed to be a look for those who are religious leaders, but there is supposed to be purity in the unseen things also. The priesthood should be honorable externally, shunning the appearance of immorality for sure, but should also be untainted internally, with righteous motives and uncorrupted intentions. Such a standard immediately indicts many of the people who consider them-

selves men and women of God. And, no, I don't speak of human im-
perfection, as even the "holiest" among us possess that. I speak more
to hidden agendas that contradict the Christ so many name-drop.

Regarding those priestly undergarments, a relevant reminder is the
conversation that's recorded in 1 Samuel between God and the
prophet Samuel. Remember that statement I mentioned in the beginning of this book, the one in which God reminded Samuel that while
man was overly concerned with appearance, God was more concerned with the hearts of men?[8] The instructions for the priests suggested that even beyond the glorious vestments they would wear, their
intentions, attitudes and even mindsets also needed to be pure.

We are told in the narrative that when they put incense in their
censers, Nadab and Abihu offered *strange fire* to God. Keep in mind
these two sons were the modern-day equivalent of church legacies. Before they were consecrated as priests, Nadab and Abihu had been
around God and God's presence. Not only were they witnesses to the
miracles God performed in Egypt in their youth, but they also were
among those who heard the voice of God with fire, lightning, smoke,
and thunder on Mt. Sinai. These sons were among those who viewed
part of God with their dad and their uncle Moses and seventy of the
church elders. They were undoubtedly familiar with God but may not
have had a mature understanding of the God they were commissioned
to serve. Even if their understanding was at full maturity, their failure
to carry out their duties appropriately showed that in some way, they
lacked discipline.

Even the most critical analyst has to acknowledge there is a significant difference between knowing *about* someone and having a personal *understanding of* that person. In the same way, there's a difference
between maintaining the necessary credentials for an assignment and
having the necessary discipline to perform the assignment effectively.

Although Nadab and Abihu were raised having been exposed to the God of Israel, and even though they had been anointed for God's service, they may have lacked the appropriate reverence for that same God. Among the chief priestly duties was the preparation of sacrifices. When sacrifices were offered, the Old Testament describes God's presence as coming down in the form of fire and consuming the sacrifices. The Levitical account details how after a seven-day period of consecration to inaugurate their service, Nadab and Abihu took it upon themselves to attempt to offer a sacrifice to God, but for some reason they were not authorized to do so.[9] Or maybe it was that they did so in an inappropriate way. To this day there is a lot of disagreement among biblical scholars about the nature of the offense in this text.

There have been many attempts to analyze the infraction of Nadab and Abihu, and analysts are conflicted as to why the sons decided to offer their own sacrifice. Almost all of the possible explanations present serious concerns. Consider just two of the possibilities. It could have been that both sons were so excited and enamored by the fire that God had sent before that they tried to get God to do it again. If that were the case, it would highlight the danger of entertaining a relationship with God only to generate excitement. Another possibility is that they were trying to impress the people, and this too is problematic, as it suggests that the sons were attempting to steal away from God the attention and glory that only God was worthy of, in which case they were similarly bound to face God's wrath.

One interpretation is that Nadab and Abihu offered "pagan incense," but the Hebrew language that the story is written in implies that the incense they burned as *strange fire* was the same incense mentioned elsewhere in the Old Testament.[10] Theologian Roland Gradwohl concluded that as duly appointed and consecrated priests, Nadab and Abihu had an absolute right to perform a sacrifice and thus must have performed their duties inappropriately.[11] The text indicates that Nadab and Abihu did have a right to sacrifice, but it's hard to conclusively say why their sacrifice was inappropriate. What should not be argued is that Nadab and Abihu were responsible for performing their duties appropriately and had the necessary training and ability to do so.

Nadab and Abihu took the bowls (censers) for the sacrifice, put incense in them, and sacrificed to God. But in doing it inappropriately, they offered *zuwr*, translated as *strange* fire before God. The swift punishment was that God sent down his own fire to kill them instantly. It is intriguing that God would allow the very same substance that these two brothers have somehow mishandled to be the instrument of their demise. Fire was a necessary phenomenon as it was a prescribed part of worship and sacrifice. When done appropriately, the fire that consumed the sacrifice would serve God's purpose and maintain the fellowship between the Lord and the people. In this case, the fire was used to express a severe consequence. And it's oh so tempting to pity the two brothers; however, the ease with which God kills them emphasizes that given the seriousness of their role and the responsibilities they carried, Nadab and Abihu should have known better. Period. No one can say they were thrust into their position without training. No one can say they weren't prepared. They went through an extensive process by which they were set apart and inaugurated into the priestly office. They were absolutely prepared for the assignment. They were absolutely trained in their responsibilities; they just failed in carrying them out.

Strange Fire in the American Priesthood

I didn't recount the story of Nadab and Abihu to focus on the two Old Testament men. I did so to highlight the problem of men and women in the priesthood mishandling their assignments. I'm speaking of the frequency of those who are called to ministry falling on the wrong side of some of the most basic of issues, and in doing so, contradicting the very same text they claim to preach from. The Levitical account suggests that although offering sacrifices to God was a part of worship, worship was (and remains) more complex than scheduled sacrifices in a temple. The idea of worship includes our way of life and can even be extended to our attitudes and ways of thinking. A pure view of worship leaves one wondering just what it is that so many American priests—American pastors, ministers, faith leaders— are worshipping. It certainly can't be God. When whole segments of evangelicalism refuse to denounce racism and simultaneously support a president who cages little children, we should be questioning the nature of the church's worship.

Elsewhere in the Bible are the words of John the evangelist, who wrote, "God is a spirit, and they that worship him must worship him in spirit and in truth."[12] I am constantly floored by the myriad clergy who speak of a holy God and yet casually approach God without regard for that holiness. And I'll be the first to admit that the nature of holiness is up for debate. For some the term refers to a particular set of Christian denominations, and for others the term represents the degree to which one aligns their life with the perceived attributes of God. For the sake of this discussion let's embrace the latter. If the goal of holiness is to be more like God, to be a better representation of God, then we need to at least endeavor to act in ways that God would act. That also means that our actions speak to our beliefs about how God acts. When the priests choose not to welcome the other (i.e., the immigrant), they're making a statement about how they believe God acts. When the priests embrace a president who acts unjustly, they're making a statement about God's view of injustice. Failures in the priesthood are just one more reason that we need prophets, but more on that later.

Nadab and Abihu failed in holiness because the nature of their assignment and the oil that was poured on them separated them. Each of us is destined for a different station in life and called to a different purpose, and many of us who embrace Christianity believe that all are established in God's plan. Though we likely have never had (and likely never will have) oil poured on us in a ceremonial fashion, we are not unlike Nadab and Abihu in possession of a call or assignment. It is ours to cherish the call and the certification process that God has taken us through. Having obtained that certification, we have a responsibility to carry out our various offices of sacrifice, being faithful to our assignments. In a day in which injustice and bigotry are on full display at the highest levels, including from the prince, it is even more critical that the priesthood take seriously its responsibilities.

Drinking the Kool-Aid

At its worst the American priesthood has produced some destructive figures. Many people forget that before he moved a mass of followers to a cult compound in the jungle of Guyana, Jim Jones was a well-known and well-liked American evangelist. He was an American priest. We know that his life, like those of his followers, ended in a well-publicized mass suicide/ mass murder, but before creating the death trap known as Jonestown, Jim Jones had the attention of many prominent individuals, including mayors, governors, and even a president. The historical record shows that just two years before the event in which he and his followers died, Jones was lauded by some of California's most prominent politicians. According to David Chidester, Jones was named among one hundred outstanding clergymen by *Religion in*

Life (1975); he was given the Humanitarian of the Year award by the *Los Angeles Herald* (1976); he even received the Martin Luther King Jr. Humanitarian of the Year award from Glide Memorial Church of San Francisco (1977).[13] None of these awards suggest a man that is a mass murderer. They are the kinds of plaques, certificates, and trophies that appear in pastors' offices across the country.

When one examines Jones's early church work, they won't find a whole bunch of glaring warning signs. Jones had a fairly typical evangelical introduction into ministry. He was ordained into the Independent Assemblies of God in 1956 and later created the People's Temple Church, which functioned like many other evangelical churches of the time.[14] Historical documents show that at one point in its early years, the church held Sunday School at 9:30 a.m. and 1:00 p.m., regular worship at 10:45 a.m., and a miracle service at 2:30 p.m. There were clearly lots of things happening at the People's Temple, and others took notice. There were other services also. There was an evangelistic service every Sunday night at 7:45 p.m. and a Thursday-evening service. Jones even had a fifteen-minute radio broadcast on Sunday mornings at 8:00 a.m. Even early on, Jones was a charismatic and well-known individual in the Indianapolis community where his ministry started, leading to his appointment to the Indianapolis Human Rights Commission in 1961.

Of course, we all know there's no rule that being a perceived humanitarian and competent church administrator prevents one from doing horrible things, either at the time of perception or in the future. In more recent times Jerry Sandusky, though not a religious leader, was viewed as a good man and a good coach, only to be exposed as a serial child molester. The various biographies of Jones and the accounts of his early leadership make one wonder if there were warning signs. Did Jones show flashes of sadism? Were there omens of evil that could've been detected early on? I don't really have an answer to that question, and there isn't enough space in this book to examine it properly. One thing that is apparent is that Jones's example is just one of many in which American religious leaders grow in power and prominence with the blessing of American political leaders, only to be revealed as unrighteous individuals.

By the early 1970s Jones had moved to San Francisco and found himself heavily involved in the community. It was in San Fran that Jones received many of the aforementioned awards, and in 1976 San Fran mayor George Moscone appointed Jones to the San Francisco Housing Authority. The Congressional record from June 1973 shows that Rep. George Brown of California commended Jones and the Temple for their contributions to the community.

By November 1978 Jim Jones had moved to Guyana and established a compound there with nearly one thousand of his followers. On November 18, 1978, at Jones's direction, more than nine hundred people committed suicide or were murdered, almost all of them American citizens. Notes from Oxford University Press's *Journal of Church and State* capture the raw impact of the event:

> The Guyanese government in early February filed suit against the People's Temple of the Disciples of Christ and two of its surviving members still in Guyana, seeking thousands of dollars in damages. The suit did not estimate the cult's local bank account and did not set a total amount of damages sought. Reportedly, the damages sought include expenses incurred in the government's cleanup following the more than nine hundred deaths.[15]

As I've examined Jim Jones over the years, the thing that has struck me most has been his interactions with Rosalyn Carter. Mind you, Jimmy and Rosalyn Carter are probably some of the closest things we have to modern-day American saints. Their lives are testaments to good works and integrity, and I think that matters. But that doesn't negate the historical record which shows that in an effort to get close to political power, Jim Jones worked his way into a friendly relationship with Rosalyn Carter.[16] In the past other faith leaders have done similar things. In the early twentieth century, Grigori Rasputin did something similar with the Romanov family, cozying up to the tsarina and eventually wielding tremendous influence within the Russian Imperial family. Jim Jones wasn't nearly as successful, but it amazes me that someone who would so prominently do great evil in just a few years had such access to the wife of one of the leaders of the free world.

These relationships speak to a sort of misidentification that we are all susceptible to. It's a kind of deception of the very elect. In different ways, both Jones and Rasputin viewed themselves as prophets, but they were really priests with immense personal flaws. Maybe the biggest flaw for each of them was their sick view of power. Some have suggested that Jones's actions were based on an ideology of redemptive sacrifice, that in calling for mass suicide he was really hoping to have an outsized impact on America's faith. One such analysis states, "Jones's ideology of redemptive sacrifice had been intentionally decentering: he argued that the Jonestown deaths would have a performative impact on America that would shake America's faith in its own centered order, an order that Jones characterized as oppressive, capitalist, fascist, and racist."[17] Such intentions suggest that Jones may have operated out of a perceived prophetic mandate. There were certainly oppressive conditions to address in his city and America at large, but other individuals and organizations were able to remain faithful to the cause of fighting such conditions without tending toward evil. Even in San Francisco, there were other churches with social justice orientations, like the Church for the Fellowship of All Peoples cofounded by Howard Thurman and Alfred Fisk. Theirs was a church that pursued interracial worship and reconciliation but never allowed such pursuits to morph into cultish adherence. Whatever Jones's intentions, he was a sick man who was unfortunately supported by domestic and foreign government leaders until those leaders possessed enough discernment to realize that he was dangerous.

I've highlighted Jim Jones to point out a persistent problem, not just in terms of race, but in terms of money, power, and influence as well. In America we continue to promote an unjust priesthood only to cry foul when that institution reveals the depth of its unrighteousness. Sure, no one person or institution is perfect, but one would've hoped that somehow, someway, someone would've been able to identify the evil in Jim Jones. No, we can't blame the people who were in government at the time for the actions of a lone religious fanatic, nor can we blame the church leaders of the time. I just wonder what is it that blinds us to the danger in our midst? What is it that causes us to see past flaws in our religious leaders and award citations to some and appoint others to commissions? What is it? Moreover, what is it that prevents so many who have a platform from speaking up when the dangers of illegitimate worship are so obvious?

THE BLACK CHURCH

There is no full understanding of the American priesthood without an examination of the black church. The only reason there is a black church is that for so long African Americans were denied the opportunity to openly worship, either by themselves or with the already established predominantly white churches. Hence today, denominations like the African Methodist Episcopal Church (AME) exist, not because their founders were determined to create black denominations, but because they had no alternative due to entrenched oppression and exclusion. Out of that oppression was birthed an institution that sustained a people and has served as the vineyard for some of black peoples' most storied laborers. Where there is religion, there are priests, and even to this day, the black priesthood represents one of the most, if not the most, important leadership element for black individuals. Of Peter Paris's four ideal types of black religious leadership, the *priestly* style was identified as being the oldest in black culture, tracing its roots all the way back to Africa.[1]

No doubt, the bedrock of the black church is black preaching. In movies, black preaching has been represented by the likes of characters like reverend Cleophus James (portrayed by James Brown) in *Blues Brothers*. Those of us who have grown up in (and are still immersed in) the culture of the black church know that there is something iconic about black preaching that renders it both entertaining and intriguing. Yet far beyond being entertaining, black preaching at its best is powerful and effective. At its best it can move the psyche and ultimately the soul of those who hear it. In the African American context, the preaching moment usually involves an intense musicality. The truth is this musicality is a lingering manifestation of the musical elements of its African roots, and through this musicality, black preaching continues to exist as not only sermon, but moment. Within the moment there is both interaction and celebration, and through the moment, the preacher in the African American context offers hope to hearers, many of whom represent historically marginalized and oppressed populations. An examination of this musicality is helpful in the pursuit of an understanding of what makes the black priesthood a distinct thing in American society.

The Black Priesthood

By itself, music is an integral component of worship in the African American tradition. Wendell J. Mapson, writing about the music ministry in many black churches, mentioned that many pastors take what he described to be a "hands-off approach to the whole area of the music ministry of the church."[2] Yet it is important to understand that observation as regarding their approach to the *formal* music ministry. The distinction is needed because it might also be said that music is in many ways a key part of the ministry of most pastors of African American churches, even if that musicality is only manifested in their preaching. While music may be a universal communication medium, it is essential to the definition of the African American worship experience. Otis Moss III, who succeeded Jeremiah Wright Jr. at Trinity United Church of Christ in Chicago, called music "the only activity that engages the entire brain."[3] In black preaching, that full-brain stimulation goes past the brain and penetrates the very soul of the congregants. Those are just some of the reasons why musicality remains a part of the black preaching tradition, and why preachers in our context minister to not only the brain of the hearers, but to the body and soul as well. The experience is what Jon Michael Spencer calls a *kratophany*, and one that historically "moved hearers away from the history that had unleashed terror upon them."[4]

There are always exceptions, but the traditional black preaching moment is an interactive experience that is at once both imperative and celebratory. It has to be celebratory, because those who hear black preaching usually represent the underrepresented, the historically oppressed, and the communities who have suffered most under American society's mistreatment. For those reasons, the tradition lingers, and likely will if the injustices and oppression we experience continue to do the same.

African Origins

The African origins of the black church represent an intensely oral *and* musical tradition. many scholars have noted the musicality of the Africans from which slaves and ultimately African Americans descended. The African (specifically West African) oral and musical tradition included storytelling, call-and-response, and many of the elements that now dominate not only black preaching, but African American worship overall. Eileen Southern notes, "The singing style employed by the Africans was characterized by high intensity . . ."[5] Indeed black preaching and singing are now known for, among other things, high intensity. It must be understood that this high intensity at its core is a vestige of the past, of the ancestral roots and historical development of the progeny that now carry the blood of those Africans.

However, one errs if they think of black preaching as somehow lacking technicality. Scientific and technical analysis of the musicality of black preaching and worship have actually been conducted. As these elements have been analyzed, many have found technical similarities between black preaching and West African folk singing. Spencer lists fluctuations in pitch and use of repetitive cadence among these connections.[6] Yet in black preaching, as in much of African American worship, there is a distinctive element of improvisation that is not common to all forms of Christian worship. Improvisation, like many of the other continuing musical elements of black preaching, can be attributed to African roots. Of course, improvisation is not just a musical technicality; it is also a device that allows for change, individual response, and even spontaneity. These are elements that many would list as some of the defining qualities of black preaching and of African American worship. Improvisation is also a quality that, for many, makes the *experience* of black preaching preferable to other styles of preaching.

Like their ancestors before them, many black preachers have long linked the distinctive preaching, prayer, and praise (song) elements of black worship in the continuance of a style unlike any other demographic segment of Christianity. Weaving all three elements is a sound, a unique musicality and intonation. Spencer writes, "That black preachers intoned their sermons and prayers is no historical novelty, for their African ancestors changed oral history and folk stories, and their African American progeny moaned bluesy hollers, and vendors whooped street cries."[7] Even today, not only in the African American preacher's preaching, but in their praying and their singing, there is a musical folk element. African American preachers are often thought of as storytellers, with sermons that are frequently narrative; prayers that, like the repentance in the 9th chapter of Nehemiah, regularly recount from whence God has already brought a group; and songs that sing of God's goodness over time. These are folk elements that are not recent innovations, but connections to a rich and ancient past.

There are other things to consider about the musical expression of the black church and what it has meant for black people. Consider that music was available to black people when literacy was not. The truth is, for centuries blacks were denied literacy by intention. Rhythm, on the other hand, could never be denied, and it was music that helped sustain a people when the ability to read and write could not. Princeton's Albert J. Raboteau notes, "Most slave preachers were hampered by illiteracy in a religion that placed such importance on the written word of the Bible."[8] Slave preachers, the original black preachers, were not allowed to read. Despite many of them having superior oratorical abilities, they lacked the formal literacy now expected of African American preachers. Songs and spirituals were readily available, to be etched upon the heart, and to be sung both in and out of the sermon. Those in the field of education note the extent to which music mnemonically aides in memorization and recall. It may have been the musical recitation of spirituals, hymns, and spiritual songs that assisted the early black preachers in the development of the style that would come to characterize black preaching.

Even the rhythmic elements, like the improvised nature of black preaching, reflect African traditions. Today, the way that many black preachers "often drum upon the podium to stress important words in key sentences" is a link to Africa.[9] History shows that at a certain point, the drumbeat of African slaves became a threat to their masters, as beyond a simple sound, the drumbeat represented a powerful communication tool. Through the creative use of drumbeats, the community could alert each other to a master's arrival or even signal a time to sneak away to worship. Still, the list of those things connecting black preaching to its ancestral roots includes other musical elements that today seem synonymous with the style.

One of the most famous musical elements of black preaching and worship is call-and-response. Call-and-response, while sometimes occurring via improvisation, is unique in that it represents specific roles on the part of multiple parties. There is a call or an initial pronouncement (in the case of the sermon, the call would come from the preacher) and a response. Regarding call-and-response, Moss writes, "It's not just people talking back to each other . . . In the talking back is a new message that's being created."[10] Moss's point must not be lost, nor should it be isolated to the element of call-and-response. The musicality of black preaching represents an experience that in and of itself is a new creation, but again, this has a history and a link to its African past. Specifically, it is related to the griot tradition of West Africa.[11] The griots were poetic storytellers who helped perpetuate the oral tradition.

Improvisation and call-and-response are both connected to what can be called *ritual freedom*. This is a term which states that "the spirit dictates, and not the printed order of worship, who shall participate, when, and for how long."[12] Ritual freedom is especially important when one considers a people with a history of marginalization and being bound. When considering the oppression that African Americans have experienced, first via their ancestors and later via lingering societal injustices, one begins to recognize where the oppressed would seek out a liberating experience. In worship, and even in the preaching moment, the rituals of worship, like those millenia before in West Africa, offered an opportunity for freedom and expression not only on the part of those who had the mic or the floor, but also to those in the audience or congregation. Raboteau hints at the historical nature of this idea: "A white minister remarked in 1863 that the 'colored brethren' are so much preferred as preachers. When in the pulpit there is a wonderful symphony between the speaker and his audience . . ."[13] That symphony is only possible if the audience is afforded the opportunity to participate.

Slave ministers held a high position and status, largely due to their ability to intertwine musical elements into their presentation. Even today, we must acknowledge the historical roots of the way many of us who are a part of the tradition of black preaching assess its success or failure. There remains an expectation in many historically African American Christian denominations that the preaching contain dynamic musical elements. There are settings where we even go so far as to deem the sermon unsuccessful when some of those elements are absent. Cleophus Larue identified the historical nature of this when he wrote (regarding call-and-response specifically), "The dynamic pattern of call and response between preacher and people was vital to the progression of the sermon, and unless the Spirit roused the congregation to move and shout, the sermon was essentially unsuccessful."[14]

At almost all points, the musical traditions and elements of black preaching can be traced to historical foundations, most of which go back much farther than the slave plantation and connect with points in ancient West Africa and beyond. I've detailed the tradition of black preaching to not only underscore its centrality to the uniqueness of the black church, but also to identify some of what validates naming the black church as its own special institution. The American priesthood is in no way a monolith. As an institution within an institution, the black church has its own segment of unjust priests and its own festering cancers that need the light of prophetic witness. Nevertheless, concerning the issue of race, it is the black church that has served as the most impactful institution on the frontlines of the fight for justice.

From this institution has risen a lingering tension between priest and prophet, as so many of America's black priests have had to also serve as prophets. That tension is necessarily a stressful one, but one that historically has helped to keep up the potency of black preaching.

The Biblical Foundation

Of course, we can't rely on history only. Like most black preaching, any apologetic for the musicality of black preaching must also connect to the Bible. It was the apostle Paul who wrote in Romans, "How, then, can they call on the one they have not believed in? And how can they believe in the one of whom they have not heard? And how can they hear without someone preaching to them? And how can anyone preach unless they are sent?"[15] The African American church continues to exalt the preacher as one who is sent. There is a sense and belief that the preacher, at any given moment, is the one who is anointed for the moment and that the Holy Spirit must work through him or her for their message to be effective. It can be said that either consciously or subconsciously, music is a part of our assessment of the Spirit's presence. Consider another passage from the book of Romans chapter 8. Paul wrote, "We do not know what we ought to pray for, but the Spirit himself intercedes for us through wordless groans."[16] Today those groans are felt in the sounds of black preaching.

William B. McClain lists biblical emphasis, prophetic preaching, poetic style, dialogue, declarative (as opposed to suggestive), and life situational as the characteristics of black preaching.[17] Music or not, there is an expectation that the Bible have a front seat in black preaching, yet the expectations are extremely high, as the Bible must somehow be poetically and musically presented. A more informative analysis as it relates to music is that of James Earl Massey, who lists as five insights from the sermons of black preaching, sermons that are functional, festive, communal, radical, and climactic.[18] There is a festive and celebratory quality that is expected as well. What makes the black sermon climactic is that "it seeks some type of celebratory close to make an impression on the hearers."[19] Spencer reminds us that even beyond the musical celebration in black preaching, God is the ultimate messenger, writing, "Musicality in black preaching operates beneath the structures of logical communication and enhances the message spoken on behalf of God."[20]

To describe contemporary black preaching, Henry Mitchell lists as "three chief characteristics of preaching in traditional African American churches," whooping, spontaneity, and an "imaginative, narrative . . ." structure.[21] *Whooping* is a pattern of musical celebratory conclusion, and it is commonly used to impress upon the hearer the heart of the narrative—the biblical narrative. Spencer goes on to say, "The music of black preaching can be understood as a sort of 'singing in the spirit,' for there is a surplus (*glossa*) expressed in music which accompanies the rational content (*logos*) enunciated in words."[22] In Spencer's analysis, we are reminded of Paul's words that "the Spirit himself intercedes for us."[23] For many, the musical rise of black preaching represents a moment in which the Spirit, through the preacher, not only speaks, but intercedes for those who would hear.

Continuity and the Present Cultural Context

As time has passed, the musical elements of black preaching have remained, and some might argue that given the current political and social climate in the United States, they are needed more than ever. There is the expectation that there be a celebratory element to black preaching, one that leaves the congregation higher than they were before they heard the message. In recalling the nature of this experience, Moss writes, "There was nothing like witnessing, not just the preacher becoming possessed by the Word, but the entire congregation reshaping the message as they affirm, push, doubt, and support the preacher, with words such as, 'Take your time,' and 'That's Right!' and with the ascent of the preacher."[24] Here the preaching moment is interactive and dynamic. Melva Costen, like others, uses the term *symphonic* to describe what occurs during the moment of black preaching. She writes, "Some preachers continue the tradition of a symphonically orchestrated form of sermonizing."[25] *Symphonically orchestrated* is a sophisticated way of saying *musical*.

It is important, however, to remember that black preaching, musical or not, continues to take place largely in the context of black theology, which Mapson describes as "how black people see God, the world, and themselves from the vantage point of the oppressed."[26] One of my mentors, Dr. Wayne E. Croft, notes that in the midst of the continuing traditions and patterns of black preaching, threats exist from what he terms "individualistic preaching, full of emotion," in which the hearers "live our life trying to make it day to day without ever being called to action to change the system."[27] That might be one drawback of an overemphasis on musicality. It may be the case that in some instances, the continuing desire to celebrate and partake of the jubilation that arises via the music of black preaching causes us to neglect the responsibility to take collective action after the sermon. As African Americans, a distinct people with a distinct history, continue to face unique challenges, it is likely that the need for a celebratory element in black preaching will remain.

The typical black preaching moment is, today, more than a moment; it is an experience, and one that goes beyond intellectual stimulation. Like the traditions of its African roots and origins, African

American homiletical musicality exists as storytelling, improvisation, call-and-response, and more. On any given Sunday morning, black preachers unite their congregations in symphonic orchestration, with the intention of not only turning hearts and minds toward biblical truths and redemptive works, but also lifting spirits out of temporary states of despair. The musicality of black preaching continues to help turn those who would be marginalized toward that which Christ offered: hope, and that via climactic musical celebration.

Hip-Hop's Critique of the Black Church

Even as preaching remains the bedrock of the black church, it is evident that the church's influence has changed. In recent decades some of the leading voices in the hip-hop community have made it a point to critique the church specifically. In the evolution of hip-hop we have an interesting parallel to the evolution of the black church. As time has passed, hip-hop's influence on the culture has increased while the black church's influence has either remained stagnant or decreased. The relationship between the two actually highlights the tension between priestly and prophetic functions. The baby boomers who served as the forefathers of hip-hop came of age at a time when black preachers were often prophetic. It's no coincidence, then, that with the decline in black prophetic preaching, we see the rise of hip-hop.

Today it can be said that hip-hop has risen to the mainstream in American culture, and the genre continues to garner increasing levels of critical analysis and scholarly attention. In recognition of hip-hop's status as a legitimate art form and major contributor to African American culture, the Smithsonian Institution dedicated a significant amount of space to the creation, evolution, and influence of hip-hop in the National Museum of African American History and Culture.

Throughout the evolution of hip-hop, some of its most recognized artists have included theological expressions in their lyrics. In recent years America's consciousness has been forced to engage social justice issues and a constant critique of the church's engagement of social justice. It is appropriate to consider how justice is and has been theologically treated by some of mainstream hip-hop's most prominent artists. Many of the biggest names in the genre have expressed the theme of justice via their lyrics over the years, but not all of them have done this theologically. Despite many hip-hop artists continuing to rap prophetically about the lack of justice in elements of American society, those artists represent a minority. Contemporary theological expressions of justice in hip-hop are much less prominent than similar expressions in the 1990s, a time when hip-hop was fighting for mainstream acceptance. The most significant difference between the hip-hop of today and that of previous years is that the artists today theologically speak of justice in a way that is less critical of the church. That epitomizes what causes once-prophetic voices to become passive ones. When voices become more mainstream and more accepted, they tend to lose their prophetic luster. There is an inverse correlation between the rise of social and cultural capital and the willingness to challenge and critique. Both the church and hip-hop bear witness to this.

Hip-Hop's Evolution

Few people today would argue that hip-hop is not a distinctive art form worthy of recognition and scholarly attention. Hip-hop, now approaching its sixth decade, is old enough that considerable developments in its evolution can be chronicled. As a genre, it has been viewed by many scholars as having been built upon the same capitalism and consumerism that has been an injustice to so many in the black community. That means that any attempts by hip-hop artists to fight for justice mean fighting against some of the same forces that have helped to popularize the genre. It is hard for music artists (of any genre) and their songs to gain mainstream notoriety when producers and executives don't believe they will appeal to a wide audience. Prophetic music that challenges the status quo is less likely to appeal to the masses than songs that promote materialism and pleasure.

Only recently has hip-hop been given broad respect and a more mature assessment. That's because the still-infantile hip-hop of the late 1980s and early 1990s was born out of the plight of the black urban communities from which it emerged. The hip-hop of those years reflected the trauma of violence, oppression, and moral decay. Contemporary hip-hop is too broad of a genre to paint with one brush. Like many other genres of music, it represents a community with varied emphases and audiences, many of which reflect the geographic regions from which the various artists emerge. At its best hip-hop serves as a means for many to poetically and musically express themselves. Also at its best, hip-hop is an art form that can even add to the church's ministry, and this is seen by the increasing embracement of hip-hop by mainline Christianity, though not always in the traditional worship setting. In his *Introduction to the Practice of African American Preaching* homiletics scholar Frank Thomas devoted a whole chapter to hip-hop's relationship to black preaching. Citing comments made to him by Valarie Bridgeman, Thomas writes:

> There is now a generation that has been raised with hip-hop music, spoken word, poetry slams, and now Gospel slam. This generation finds the poetic a natural form of speech in proclamation. Her [Bridgeman's] concern was that they would come to believe that there is no place in the church for their poetic form of proclamation. She said the church is put off by the profane language and does not realize how

sacred this generation believes life is, despite the vulgar ways they talk about it.[28]

The vulgarity associated with hip-hop has been a flashpoint for many black church leaders, and one can argue they are justified in their skepticism of the genre. Frederick L. Ware writes of what hip-hop can be at its worst. "At its worst, hip-hop exudes a hedonistic spirit and oppositional outlook which challenges conventional Christian morality."[29] Too often the more negative side of hip-hop is the one portrayed in the media.

Opposition to hip-hop is rarely focused on the art form itself; rather opposition is usually focused on the questionable morals associated with hip-hop culture. It is sad that many of those who dismiss the legitimacy of hip-hop, especially in the Christian community, are sons and daughters of the movements from which it was born. Hip-hop as we know it today is the child of the period of stagnating progress that arose in the wake of decades of protest. Consider one of the most famous hip-hop artists, Tupac Shakur. Tupac was born into a family with extensive roots in the Black Panther organization and Black Power movement. The struggle for justice was in Tupac's blood, but he was graced with an artistic ability that provided a special vehicle for expressing his frustration with the plight of black youth in America. Tupac also found a way to express his theology in his music, as he sought justice from the American government and society at large. Speaking of the genre broadly, he described hip-hop music as "a reaction to the failures and the fallacies of the so-called civil rights movement."[30] Tupac, speaking in the 1990s, was referring to how many in the hip-hop movement felt like some of the objectives of the civil rights movement and its leaders were left unachieved. The hip-hop music of that time reflects those feelings.

Interpretations of Hip-Hop by Religion Scholars

Irrespective of perceptions of hip-hop in the church context, the genre still contends with an overall negative reputation. Ware notes that "uninhibited expressions of sexuality, confrontational human behavior, and outlaw identities are dominant aspects of global hip-hop culture."[31] As economics have become more globalized, so too has hip-hop culture. Although things like gangster activity, misogyny, and violence represent only segments of hip-hop culture, those are the images that still dominate the external perception of the genre.

There are also unfortunate stereotypes about the generation that is now most associated with hip-hop. In religious studies, some have called the millennial generation (those born in 1981–1996) the hip-hop generation, since it is the generation that has grown as hip-hop has come into the mainstream.[32] It is not uncommon to hear within seminary walls or read in magazines and on blogs assertions that those in the millennial, or hip-hop, generation are leaving the church. The scholarship does not completely support that assertion. Joy K. Challenger addresses that misconception, stating, "Despite the rumors . . . researchers find it difficult, based on the data, to conclude that emerging adults in the United States have as a group become less religious or more secular in the last quarter century."[33] The increasing influence of hip-hop on young people cannot be taken as the decreasing influence of the church on those same young people. However, it is true that the church has been hostile to hip-hop in the past, focusing on the questionable morality.

The youngest third of the millennial generation has grown up with social media, and in the same way, hip-hop has grown up with the music video as a means of spreading its message.[34] Video has allowed those artists who choose to include theology in their lyrics to also visu-

ally express those themes, rendering their messages even more powerful. Otis Moss III is one preacher who has actively sought to analyze
hip-hop's place in the black church, and he proclaimed, "The black
church is now in the post soul generation—the first generation that
does not have all its roots in the church."[35] Moss identified one of the
central challenges of the embrace of hip-hop by the church, which is
the genre's non-church roots. Hip-hop came about partially due to
frustration with movements that had been church led. As a result, hip-
hop and the church have historically been at odds with one another.

Hip-Hop's Connection to the Black Priesthood

Despite both institutions being at odds in the past, the paths of hip-
hop and the black church are beginning to cross more. The former
represents an art form that is uniquely associated with the core con-
stituency of the latter. Hip-hop is without a doubt one of the foremost
vehicles of expression for black youth, and the black church is still, as
Ware writes, "the central institution in African American communities. However, it is unlikely to have this centrality in the realm of politics and culture."[36] An additional piece of evidence to support Ware's
caveat about the realm of politics and culture is the fact that prophetic
hip-hop is still able to challenge the status quo with or without the
church's involvement.

Interestingly, the same capitalism and consumerism in hip-hop I
mentioned above has also become a problem in the black church.
Ware writes, "Capitalism and consumerism have the effect of bending
all cultural institutions, including Christian churches, toward materialism."[37] The desire to market hip-hop to the mainstream has caused
it to move in the direction of materialism. This contrasts with the early
forms of hip-hop which were more organic expressions of life for
blacks in places like the Bronx. Thomas Kane suggests that the organic

expression of hip-hop is "the real" or what Frank Thomas describes as "an existentially authentic performance," for certainly, "To be real is to rap about a reality and live the reality that one is rapping about."[38] Like hip-hop, the church has unfortunately moved in the direction of materialism, as various platforms, not the least of which is television, have given charismatic individuals the ability to promote prosperity Gospel.

Challenger identified some practices of the black church which are relevant to a discussion of hip-hop's connection to the black church. Challenger seems to question much of hip-hop's ability to express the Christian faith. She suggests that the exemplary Christian disciple is committed to a life of worship (in both corporate participation and private practice); engaged in service to others; and engaged in social justice/action.[39] As stated above, part of the origin of hip-hop is a response to the perceived failures of previous movements. Those movements were largely led by the church. Some might view it as hypocritical for the church to, on the one hand, deny hip-hop's ability to express the Christian faith due to a failure in one or more areas of discipleship, yet on the other hand fail to fully live out its own walk of discipleship by lacking engagement in social justice.

A younger generation, a hip-hop generation if one likes that term, may be questioning why the black church, which at one time led the effort for social justice for black individuals, is now so absent from the fight for social justice. The generation preceding hip-hop's creation fought against segregation, earned the right to vote, and helped bring about the death of Jim Crow. Challenger writes of how this work "led to political and social activism expressed in marches, boycotts, and other forms of protest. Yet there was disillusionment among younger Christians, similar to today, dissatisfied with how their churches were or were not involved in the fight for equality (and justice)."[40] Many of the young people of the late 1980s and 1990s viewed hip-hop as a ve-hicle for them to engage in the work of social justice. Today, while church acceptance of hip-hop may have generally increased, the ac-ceptance has not translated into increased emphasis on social justice for the church members.

One final consideration regarding hip-hop and the black church is social media. Social media has not only changed the nature of the Christian community, but it has also changed the way the hip-hop generation engages the black church. Ware writes, "The youth are in-creasingly organizing in social media (i.e., Facebook, Twitter, etc.) in-stead of the church . . . The downside of the churches' use of social media is the absence of exemplars in prophetic ministry and social jus-tice."[41] The irony is that the same social media that has led to the in-creasing focus of the church on material things has also led to an in-crease in youth engagement in social justice. Hip-hop just happens to be one of the means through which those young people are engaging in the work.

Hip Hop's Evolving Concern with Justice

Whether current mainstream hip-hop artists realize it or not, their genre is uniquely connected to the struggle for justice. According to Ibram Kendi, "hip-hop and rap blossomed in 1988 after a decade of growth from the concrete of the South Bronx."[42] As the melody of hip-hop became more defined, the lyricists discovered, particularly in the late 1980s, that they could use the musical platform of hip-hop to con-vey their messages. As the 1980s progressed, and those in America's inner cities became increasingly *oppressed*, some hip-hop artists began to use their music to express their desire to see justice in their commu-nities. A few of them invoked theology to express their desire for justice in their community. When we speak of justice, we mean, at least in the

New Testament, something that is "reciprocal, eschatological, and compensatory."[43] Challenger goes on to identify compensatory justice as "the moral process of correcting injury, dispossession, exploitation, and the violations of rights of individuals."[44]

One of the first uniquely theological expressions of justice in main-stream hip-hop came from the group Arrested Development. On their 1992 song "Fishin' 4 Religion," the group stated:

The reason I'm fishin' 4 a new religion
Is my church makes me fall asleep
They're praising a God, that watches you weep
And doesn't want you to do a damn thing about it
When they want change the preacher says, "Shout it"
Does shout bring about change? I doubt it
All shout does is make you lose your voice[45]

Some subsequent lines make it clear that the group is responding to a lack of justice in their community, but they do so by critiquing the church's response. Their cry for justice indicts the church's work, implying that the church is more concerned with helping the community "cope" with its current condition than working to change its current condition.

No hip-hop artist had a more prophetic impact than Tupac Shakur. Among Tupac's prophetic lyrics were some that used intense theology to express a desire for justice. His use of religion has been well-documented. Tupac was also explicit in his critique of what he believed to be an oppressive American society, and like Arrested Development in "Fishin 4 Religion," he offered much critique of the church. Like other rap artists, "Tupac used quasi-religious themes in his lyrics to express his frustration with American society and his condemnation of the religious establishment."[46]

In his song "Shed So Many Tears" Tupac's very first lines were, "I shall not fear no man but God / Though I walk through the valley of death / I shed so many tears / If I should die before I wake / Please God walk with me / Grab a nigga and take me to Heaven."[47] The first lines convey the deep connection Tupac had to religion. Later in the song Tupac alluded to social problems like alcoholism, addiction to painkillers, and deaths due to violence. This Tupac song is less a call for justice, and more an expression of the lack of justice.

In another one of his songs, "Blasphemy," Tupac again identified a lack of justice, but the song on the whole is more critical of his own community. In the song, he called out drug dealers, lazy community members, and absentee fathers. He did it all by again invoking his theology. Tupac said, "Love for them that steal in the name of the Lord / Dem a tell 'nough lie but holding my bird in a cloud / Using the name of the Lord in vein / While the people in the ghetto, feel 'nough pain."[48] Like the lyrics mentioned above, this is another song that is critical of the church. As with others, Tupac's desire for justice was connected to a theology that is largely separate from the church. Tupac's conception of justice for the community might actually be one that limits the black church's role.

Tupac was writing in the 1990s, and since that time black culture has changed and, in many ways, assimilated to the dominant culture. One of the greatest changes in black culture has been the changing role of the church and black theology. According to Neal, "Contemporary African American culture is a moral and cultural challenge to the very logic of black liberation theology."[49] Black culture now includes a black theology that is much less political than it was in the past. These changes have manifested in various subgenres of hip-hop music. On the subgenre of gangsta rap, Michael Eric Dyson suggested it was "allegedly the most antipolitical of hip-hop's genres."[50] Yet gangsta rap has never represented the totality of hip-hop.

For better or for worse, Kanye West is not only a transformative figure in hip-hop; but he also happens to be a transformative figure as far as expressing theology. Kanye's work is full of references to God, but Kanye does little to advance the cause of justice. When one takes into account his political expressions in recent years, Kanye appears to harm the cause of justice. In October 2018, in just one example of his erratic political displays, Kanye met with President Trump in the Oval Office, saying of his support for Trump, "What I need *Saturday Night Live* to improve on and what I need liberals to improve on: If he don't look good, we don't look good . . . This is our president. He has to be the freshest, the flyest."[51] Unfortunately, Kanye's overt support of Trump and controversial statements on America's racial history detract from his latest efforts to promote his faith via his special Sunday Service choir performances. When Kanye's "Jesus Walks" was released in 2005, it caused significant buzz with many surprised that he would include such overtly religious themes in a secular hip-hop song. On the track West raps, "I don't think there is nothing I can do now to right my wrongs (Jesus walks with me) / I want to talk to God, but I'm afraid because we ain't spoke in so long (I want Jesus)."[52]

One of the most intriguing and prophetic voices in hip-hop is a young Chicago protégé of Kanye by the name of Chance the Rapper. Chance is the product of a deeply Christian family and is now arguably the most overtly theological mainstream hip-hop artist. What makes Chance so intriguing is that he has achieved his fame without signing to any label—his entire career, he has self-released his music. Kylee C. Smith, who like Chance is a millennial, writes, "He is a Christian like I am, but he does not make traditional 'Gospel' music . . . When I listen to Chance, it is clear that he is worshipping God through his art."[53] One could write an entire book on Chance and theology. In one of his most popular songs, "How Great," Chance has a choir begin the track with the song "How Great Is Our God." He goes on to say: "Hosanna Santa invoked and woke up slaves from Southampton to Chatham Manor."[51] I believe the reference to slaves can be interpreted as a subtle expression of Chance's view of what justice means for his community.

Chance's album *Coloring Book* is laden with Christian references, directly quoting Bible passages. Each of the Bible references is used to impress a different point, but at least a few of them are expressing a desire for justice. On his song "Blessings," Chance says: "I don't make songs for free, I make 'em for freedom / Don't believe in kings, believe in the Kingdom.[55] On the song "All We Got," Chance says: "I get my word from the sermon / I do not talk to the serpent / That's the holistic discernment."[56] Chance, in referencing the serpent that Eve encountered in the Garden of Eden, alludes to the temptation to do and support evil. It is hard to argue that hip-hop is now a mainstream art form in American culture. This genre, now old enough to warrant it, continues to receive increasing levels of scholarly attention. Although it began in the Bronx, it has grown to become a global phenomenon. From Arrested Development, to Tupac, to Kanye, to Chance the Rapper, mainstream hip-hop artists have at points expressed deep theological concepts in their work, and some of them have expressed a desire for justice. Today, there are fewer rappers using their platform to call out the church. In fact, we find Kanye (and those who join him) making some attempts to emulate or even join the church. In a digital age like the one we live in, Kanye Sunday Services, in which he convenes masses of young people to sing Gospel music, give the church much to think about. It remains to be seen if Kanye's services will last. That is to ask, as much as they are a thing now, will they continue to be a thing in a few years? It also remains to be seen if Kanye's model of church will cause change in traditional black churches. Whatever the answer to those questions may be, I still believe that of the artists who have or continue to rap prophetically, Tupac Shakur stands as one of the most prophetic rappers in the history of hip-hop. I'll concede Tupac was around at a different time, with different needs, but maybe a Tupacian prophetic critique of the church is just what the church needs. Hip-hop generations of the past took up the issue of justice with a theological verve that is missing from most hip-hop artists today. I believe that if justice once again became a central theme in hip-hop, the church would follow suit.

Black Prince vs. Black Priests

In some ways Barack Obama was a hip-hop president. He was suave, he was a gen X child of the 70s, and he understood the language of hip-hop—we know this because he used it. Barack Obama had to address the concerns of a hip-hop generation when he delivered his "More Perfect Union Speech." The speech was delivered at a time in the 2008 campaign when the issue of race was squarely at the forefront.[57] The genesis of the race talk was the media's discovery of video recordings of Obama's former pastor, reverend Jeremiah Wright Jr., delivering two sermons, one from 2001 titled "The Day of Jerusalem's Fall" and the other from 2003 titled "Confusing God and Government." The most controversial excerpt, and the one which received the most media attention, was a segment of the 2003 sermon in which Wright used expletives to describe the United States and was heard saying, "God damn America!"[58] In the sermon, Wright also made what some would consider inflammatory remarks regarding white Americans, although it should be recognized that Wright's remarks included a whole lot of factual historical content that simply can't be denied. Take for instance one paragraph of his sermon that delves into the way he believes Americans confuse God and government (emphasis mine):

> We believe God approved segregation. We believe God approved apartheid, and a document says "all men are created more equal than other men"—and we're talking about *white* men. We confuse God and government. We believe that God approves of 6 percent of the people on the face of this earth controlling all of the resources on the face of this earth while the other 94 percent live in poverty and squalor, while we give trillions of dollars of tax breaks to the *white* rich. We believe God was a founding member of the World Bank and the International Monetary Fund. Look at the lily-*whiteness* of the G-7 nations the next time you see a picture, and you tell me if you see anything wrong with that picture.[59]

To a white individual who is looking to find fault in Rev. Wright's sermon, it is easy to take such remarks out of context or consider them offensive. Others of us, especially those of us who are very familiar with the tone and tenor of black preaching, know that such strong language is somewhat commonplace in our context, and that a huge disservice is done if those remarks are taken out of context.

In response to the Wright controversy, Obama used his speech not only to condemn the remarks of Rev. Wright, but also to broaden the conversation and touch on more deep-set issues of race in America. It was not by coincidence that Obama chose to begin his speech by reminding his audience of the Declaration of Independence and the Constitution, as well as the deficiencies in both documents. In fact, the speech was delivered at Philadelphia's National Constitution Center, just yards away from where both documents were signed. In the speech he was very clear that although both documents were strong statements of purpose and declarations of liberties, they each contained errors, particularly when it came to the differing treatment of blacks and whites. Obama even stated that the Constitution was "not enough" to provide the things that were actually outlined in it. Obama didn't hide his feelings on our nation's honored texts, nor did he shy away from how unfairly those texts have treated many citizens. Nevertheless, he was also careful to remind his audience that all Americans, irrespective of race, hold "common hopes," and it was on that theme of common hopes that he extended his remarks. I'm persuaded that Obama's decision to focus on a common objective, or to offer a common appeal, is precisely what has separated him from many other politicians and speaks to what enabled him to become the first African American elected to the presidency. Obama had the expertise to state directly that race was an issue in the campaign, while simultaneously striking a much more moderate and consensus-building tone.

After Obama briefly discussed the history of race in America, and acknowledged that a race problem still existed, he proceeded to discuss the black church at length. As someone who has spent his entire life in the context of a black church experience, I can understand how an outsider might find many of the expressions inappropriate, if not radical. Here again, however, Obama was able to use the speech to demonstrate his rhetorical and philosophical proficiency. Obama took the conversation on the black church—its loud expressions of emotion, its shouting, its singing, and its dancing—and conveyed the positive impact that the black church experience has on its congregations and communities. In addition, Obama expressed how his black church experience, through the guidance of Rev. Wright, led him to a deeper relationship with Jesus Christ and to refine his faith. At the same time Obama discussed how "the most segregated hour of the week is Sunday morning," explaining that within the context of church, many intolerances and ignorant practices are sustained.

For all of his introductory and beginning remarks, the most powerful part of Obama's speech was probably the section in which he lectured on anger within the black community, and what he called resentment in the white community. As a black man I have always found it interesting that Obama used the word *anger* when talking about and discussing blacks, and the word *resentment* when discussing the feelings of whites. I believe that in referencing the anger of blacks, Obama was trying to remove some of the spirit of victimization that still lingers in the black community. Essentially, he was calling out blacks, describing their anger at the lack of privilege, which serves as a good historical note, but also as a rebuke for today. In discussing resentment in the white community, Obama accurately described the feelings that many white Americans experience when they are made to feel responsible for things they have no control over. Surely all whites are not responsible for the disparity between the education the typical black child receives and the one most white children receive. In addition, no one can hold all whites responsible for the racism that still exists within the criminal justice system. Those are just two very blunt examples of situations or ideas that feed resentment within the white community regarding race issues.

Yes, the "A More Perfect Union" speech was focused on race in America, but it also foreshadowed the relationship that Barack Obama would have with the black church. During the Clinton years, if you closed your eyes and listened to the president, you might think for a second that the Clintons were members of a black church. My personal testimony is that I can recall many times growing up watching Bill Clinton or Hillary Clinton seated on the pulpit of some black church. Bill Clinton demonstrated comfort speaking to black congregations, displaying the characteristic extemporaneous delivery that so many black preachers display Sunday after Sunday. Despite clearly being culturally black, and beloved by the black community, President Obama never quite displayed the same comfort in the black church setting. At the time that his speech on race was delivered, never before had such a major political figure in the United States used such an immense platform to flesh out the nuance of race in our society. Obama, in describing these angers and resentments, touched on extremely sensitive and controversial issues, and it was overall well-received. There is no doubt that the speech left a mark on the history of US race relations, but there is also no doubt that the speech was a little bit of a slap in the face to the black church. Although it was done indirectly, by taking the path of political expediency and throwing Rev. Wright under the bus, Obama effectively took a position on the black church, and as we look, that position was largely held throughout his eight years in the White House.

AMAZING GRACE

Black Funeral Rites

Traditions and practices surrounding death vary from culture to culture and region to region. Myriad things, including historical development, religious outlook, and even popular culture affect the death-related beliefs and rituals of any particular people. African Americans are especially distinct in their death practices. From attitudes toward death to funeral observances, the African American tradition represents a system of both historical development and Western assimilation. Sure, like preaching and worship in the black church, the traditional funeral practices of African Americans reflect West African ancestral roots as well as the story of violence and struggle involving their fight for equality. Still, influences from the black church have shaped their traditions the most.

Like so much of black history and culture, in order to understand the African American death experience, one has to go back to Western Africa. The American slave trade was conducted primarily from the West African coast, which is why many scholars believe that most African Americans are descendants of West African peoples. Those findings are confirmed by the study of modern burial rituals and practices, in which scholars have observed a significant amount of West African origin and influence. Ronald Barrett wrote that "contemporary African American funeral rites and practices are a fusion of traditional African and Western psychocultural influences."[1] African Americans observe the passing of loved ones with elements of both West African and

117

Western style. The *jazz funeral*, which is still practiced by some in the Deep South (mainly New Orleans), is directly tied to West African customs.[2] The jazz funeral involves a band and as the title indicates, jazz music. The entire structure of a jazz observance is based around the music, which as we'll see is not too different from the archetypal African American funeral. Even the penchant of African Americans to choose ground burial over cremation or other methods of disposing of a body stems from African tradition.[3] Within these practices we observe the way that thousands of miles of separation and even hundreds of years of history have not been able to break the ancient influence of West Africa on contemporary customs.

That African Americans still retain many of the traditions birthed in Africa is a testament to the endurance of those customs. The largest hurdle to those customs was slavery itself. Not only did slavery force African Americans to have to deal with death to a greater extent, but it also forced them to maintain and observe their customs in secrecy. Even before many of the early slaves arrived in the Americas, they had likely already experienced a significant amount of death. Beyond the horrible immoral and abusive realities of slavery, servitude did not allow the African descendants the opportunity to openly observe their customs. This era and the challenges it presented to blacks as a people helped to forge a certain style of African American death tradition. Karla Holloway notes that "so many blacks died untimely deaths that funeral anguish came to be rehearsed as a dimension of the culture's engaged ritual rather than as the reason for the occasion."[4] Holloway's comments highlight that the anguish of the experience of slavery began to lend itself to anguish manifested in the mourning style of the people. The emotional and expressive style with which African Americans today mourn their dead is partially a product of the experience of slavery.

For most blacks at the time, observing funeral practices while enslaved was a challenge. According to Jacqueline S. Thursby, "For the slaves living on plantations, permission to conduct a funeral ceremony was required, but it was not always granted."[5] In the event that permission was granted, the slaves would have had to conduct funeral observances with both limited time and means. The same expressive and emotional forces that dominate African American funerals today would have influenced the slaves' observances. In a special 2003 report in *The State* Pat Berman wrote, "Slaves often were forbidden from having burial services for other slaves, so they would secretly meet in the dead of the night, in the middle of a field or woods, for services."[6] Even if the authorities did not grant permission—which they often did not—it is not a stretch to assume that denial of permission would have only strengthened the communal bond and heightened the emotions of the people. The act of meeting in the dead of the night and working as a team to honor a loved one would have expressed a communal quality of African American mourning that still exists to this day.

Mournful drumbeats demonstrated many of the key elements of the African American funeral experience, including music, emotional exuberance, and group participation, as the procession with drums would have involved many congregants. The exuberant characteristic of African American funerals exists as a direct result of the painful history of the people as a race. With regard to the way African Americans approach death, Bert Hayslip and Cynthia Peveto wrote, "Attitudes and behaviors of African Americans toward death need to be understood with reference to the struggle, violence, suppressed anger, and exploded aggression that have followed."[7] Struggle and violence are not new to the African American experience; they were inherent in the experience of slavery and have existed disproportionately within African American communities since that time.

Sadly, even today, much of the African American funeral experience is still being shaped by violence. As if it were not enough to have a history forged by abuse and slavery, African Americans still must disproportionately deal with violence. Thursby wrote, "Faith in things unseen has been taught with power and consistency in black churches," alluding to the fact that this disproportionate faith in things unseen is related to the disproportionate relationship that blacks have to violence—at least as it relates to their customs related to death.[8] The communal nature of African American mourning has always intensified already intense situations. Such has been the case in the deaths of popular black figures, where blacks have openly expressed their grief for many of these famous individuals en masse. Post-slavery African Americans had to deal with a century of discrimination, Jim Crow laws, lynching, and other violent acts that only increased the exposure of blacks to death. When young Emmett Till was murdered, his mother famously insisted on having an open casket to show the world what Emmett's killers had done to him. A simple Google image search will produce pictures of Till's distorted body, badly beaten and almost unrecognizable from similar search results of his childhood pictures. Although Till's mother may not have known it at the time, her desire for the world to see her son's body serves as a perfect example of the African American mourning experience given the circumstances. Not only did Till have a ground burial after a church funeral, but he also had an open casket (despite the condition of his body), and he clearly had a very emotional send-off.

In surveys African Americans have reported "significantly more contact with victims of homicides, accidents, and wartime deaths" than other groups.[9] A more extensive study of African American death rates would most likely reveal that African Americans' death rates are higher than other groups'. Even still, that overexposure to death has contributed to an attitude of invulnerability or indifference within the African American community. The authors of one study speculated, "The conflict for survival by African Americans might have been so intense that an overt admission of vulnerability had to be denied."[10] The struggle for survival in the African American community is part of what has made the African American death customs. For African Americans the struggle and the violence have only served to reinforce the importance of community and faith in the death ritual. The history of struggle has conditioned the African American community to view death as a release of sorts, and as we will continue to see, the expressions of the grieving process reflect that perception of death as a release from life on Earth, along with the struggle and violence life on Earth brings.

The historical background and context of the African American experience lay the groundwork for analyzing the traditions that still exist within the community. In these traditions, we see the West African roots at work, as well as the influences of the slavery struggle. There is general agreement that even though the African American death experience remains distinct from the experiences of other races, there can be no doubt those Western influences have allowed that experience to develop and change. Furthermore, there are diversities within the African American death experience. As noted earlier, although now rare, some in the Deep South still practice jazz funerals, some out of novelty, others out of tradition. In addition, there are very clear geographic diversities in mourning traditions.

In nineteenth-century America, blacks demonstrated much of the community traditions and values that lingered from their African ancestry and were developed through generations in servitude. To this day the community nature of the African American death experience remains. Community participation not only reinforces solidarity and tradition, but it also helps to provide the grieving family with a source of comfort and support. There is an unspoken belief that the more friends and loved ones physically present, the more moral and spiritual support there is. In addition to being physically present, friends and loved ones will take food to the bereaved family so the grievers don't have to deal with the stress of preparing their own meals. Such practices are not unlike shiva, practiced by members of the Jewish faith. The food tradition is a sort of ritual, and as an expected ritual, it helps to reinforce the community aspect of the death process.[11] Food appears again in the African American death experience immediately following the funeral service. Most of the time, after the funeral, the family and friends have a repast. The repast is simply a meal, but more important than the meal (some would call it a feast) is the expected round of laughter, conversation, and memory sharing that occurs.

Traditions like the repast cross many borders, including religious and secular. Regardless of whether a funeral is held in a church or a funeral home, there is likely to be a repast after the service. As time has progressed, African Americans solidified as a race many more of the practices that typify their funerals today. Holloway notes, "In the 1900s it was traditional in African American communities to leave the casket open for viewing sometimes during the wake and church services."[12] Open casket funerals are the norm for African Americans. The exact origins of this tradition are unclear, but it has become just that, a tradition. Whether the complete funeral arrangements include a wake in the home and a funeral, or just a funeral, there is usually an open casket for a significant part of the arrangements. In addition, church funerals typically include time for viewing the body both before and after the service. Any latter viewing is usually more structured (mostly because it is normally the final viewing.) Mourners expect that when they go to a funeral, barring a dismemberment or cremation, they will be able to see the body one last time, and depending on their relationship with the family of the deceased, they may even be able to touch the body.

African American funerals take on slightly different tones depending on their geographic locations. Southern black funerals tend to reflect more African roots, and Northern black funerals tend to reflect more modern influences.[13] Those differences, of course, reflect broader societal differences between the Northern and Southern regions of the United States. However, regarding traditions we can see both West African and Western influences on Afro-Caribbean funeral practices as well. One major similarity between the death practices of African Americans and Afro-Caribbeans is the practice of delaying the funeral. African Americans are notorious for having funerals up to a week or ten days after the deceased has passed away, yet what few people realize is that this practice originally stems from the need for relatives and loved ones to be able to attend the funeral. Delaying the funeral gives time not only for family, friends, and loved ones to attend and participate, but it also gives all of those various stakeholders an opportunity to fulfill their function within the death system, whether it is bringing food, comforting the family, or even sometimes participating in the funeral arrangements.

Delaying the funeral has also most likely contributed to the degree to which African American children are exposed to funerals. The delay most likely gives families an opportunity to take children with them to funerals. Michael Leming and George Dickinson note that all of the social practices of blacks with regard to funerals apply to their children as well. "Young black children are routinely taken to funerals and encouraged to interact with family members who are dying in the home."[14] Exposure to death is something that many black children have at an early age. The combination of the community nature of the

African American death experience and the high levels of religious involvement provide a situation where black children are taught extensively about death practices earlier than children of other races. That exposure and teaching probably leads to the perceptions that adult blacks have about death. Blacks have concrete views toward death, most likely forged by their exposure to death at young ages.[15] A more extensive study of funeral preparations would most likely show that African Americans are more likely to make detailed funeral preparations. Such findings would lend a partial explanation to the degree to which African Americans tend to profess a certain level of comfort with death, but I contend that it simply relates to the high level of exposure.

As one studies African American history, especially with death and violence in mind, as well as the traditions that have shaped their funeral practices, it is impossible to avoid a study of African American religion. Peveto and Hayslip found that blacks tend to perceive themselves as more religious than others who share their ethnicity.[16] That religious identification is only directed at others within their own race, but even that response suggests that religion may play a particularly significant role in this race's identity. Such a high acceptance of life is directly related to the influence of the black church on both African American death concepts and practices. The same results reveal that 40 percent of African Americans find support during a crisis of death and dying in religion and church, compared to 25 percent or less for most other races.[17]

As has been stated, the black church is distinct for its style, exuberance, exhortations, loudness, looseness, and overall emotionalism. It is no coincidence that we have already identified most of those characteristics as part of the African American death experience. However, beyond emotionalism, the black church has been the single most influential force on the African American death experience. The black church has managed to tie the violent experience of the African American past with tradition, to fulfill a necessary social function in both uplifting and instructing survivors of the deceased during times of death. Leming and Dickinson found that "a strong religious background in most African American families helps to develop a belief about survival after death that makes death less threatening than it is for the more secularized white middle class."[18] Without the prospect of life after death there is no joyous celebratory service or repast filled with laughter. The beliefs instilled in African Americans by the black church—or at least someone instructed by the black church—have guided the community to develop customs that uplift life rather than elevate death.

The same belief system that gave comfort to the grieving was a belief system that gave comfort to those living under systems of social inequality and sometimes civil unrest, and naturally these doctrines had an impact on death practices. As has already been stated, struggle is a large part of the African American story, and the black church in America has always reflected that. In her study of African American mourning, Karla Holloway deals extensively with the black church, writing, "The church honored its historical role of bringing final perspectives to lives lived long and courageously . . . and to those lives cut short often, too often."[19] Yet Holloway also acknowledges the broader functions of the black church for African Americans, even beyond funerals. She writes, "The experiences brought to the sanctuary were draped in the anguished dramas of race in America."[20] Those dramas required resolution and comfort. Only the black church was able to fully provide the level of comfort that congregants needed. It was able to provide that comfort in many different circumstances, including death. Sociologist W. E. B. Dubois called the black church the "social center of Negro life."[21] Perhaps the black church was not only the social center of Negro life because it was the place where people gathered together; perhaps it was the social center because of its ability to actually socialize people. More or less that's what the black church has done: it has socialized people, inspiring them to believe that there is something better than their present circumstances and inspiring them to do things they would not otherwise do based upon faith. The black church has consistently offered oppressed persons hope and optimism about the prospect of a life in Heaven, void of the struggles and violence found here on Earth.

In addition to the fundamental belief system instilled in most African Americans by the black church is the worship style of the black church itself. In most religious traditions, funeral services and burial customs are an extension of worship styles. Some denominations consider death practices *rites* or *sacraments*. The black church is no exception. African American funerals embody the spirit of the black church. The musical spirit and passionate enthusiasm are what distinguishes the black church from other religious traditions. Even the most conservative (in terms of worship style) of the mainline predominantly black denominations still represent worship styles that involve louder music, more crowd participation, and more impassioned speaking than other denominations.

The African American death experience can include long funerals, and most African American funerals held in churches are considered a homegoing. *Homegoing* refers to the fact that the deceased is thought to be returning home to be with God. That theme is reflected in every part of the service, from the music, to the spoken word. As prominent black figures have passed away in the public eye and their funerals have been broadcast on live television, the outside world has learned that African American funerals tend to be long—much longer than a funeral program would indicate. Examples of such funerals include those of Dr. King, Thurgood Marshall, Ron Brown, Rosa Parks, Coretta Scott King, James Brown, Whitney Houston, and Aretha Franklin (Franklin's August 2018 funeral lasted eight hours). Holloway described the distinctiveness as witnessed in the funeral services of some of these leaders. "Although a national mourning was engaged and orchestrated with these state occasions, the services for King, Marshall, and Brown did not lose their black specificity, which was apparent in the music."[22] While a lot of the length comes from the personal tributes of friends and family members, and while some of the length is added by the sermon—which can take longer depending on the speaker—by and large, the funeral service is extended most by the rousing singing and celebration.

The traditional music of the African American funeral alone represents the defining characteristics of the black church; African American funerals tend to be opportunities for many traditional songs to be invoked, especially when the deceased is an elderly person or a prominent person. Many of the traditional hymns of the black church represent themes of freedom, rebirth, or heavenly reward. Songs like "I'll Fly Away" and "Come unto Me" represent standard verses with rousing choruses that usually have the entire crowd joining in song. For instance, the first verse of Albert E. Brumley's "I'll Fly Away" rings, "Some glad morning, when this life is o'er, I'll fly away / To a home on God's celestial shore, I'll fly away." The concept of a "glad morning" typifies the ideas expressed in the black church regarding death. Allusions like "flying away" or "going home" translate Christian beliefs into expressive phrases that both uplift the life of the deceased and give comfort to the family. The services are called homegoings because it is believed that the deceased has finally reached the other life. The hymn "Jacob's Ladder," which refers to the vision of a ladder experienced by the biblical figure Jacob (Israel), ends with a verse that exclaims, "Rise, shine, and give God the glory." The final verse repeats those words, evoking thoughts of victory and bliss in the presence of God. Songs of that type typify the music and the celebratory nature of many African American funerals. Although the influences from West Africa linger in the funeral practices of African Americans, there can be no doubt that it is the black Church that has the greatest effect on the character and style of African American death practices today.

Finding Grace

At no time during the Obama presidency did the roles of prince and priest overlap more than on June 26, 2015, during the nationally televised funeral for reverend Clementa Pinckney. Pinckney was an African Methodist Episcopal (AME) pastor who also served as a South Carolina state senator. Prior to his service in the state Senate, Pinckney served for four years in the state House of Representatives, having first been elected at age twenty-three as the youngest elected African American in the legislature's history. Rev. Pinckney and eight others lost their lives on June 17 of that year, when a twenty-one-year-old white supremacist planted himself in Pinckney's church and opened fire on those gathered for Bible study. It is hard for me to write this without becoming emotional, because so many elements of the tragic death of Pinckney and his members speak to the historic struggles for African Americans in this country. The church is supposed to be a safe space, as I'm sure all of those gathered on that evening felt their church was. Pinckney has become a personal hero for me, as he was one of those preachers who understood his simultaneous call to both impact public policy and pulpit ministry. An additional point of emotion for me is the reality that black people are expected to be welcoming and affirming, only to be harmed by those they welcome. The young murderer, even with his wicked intentions, was welcomed into the church and allowed to sit and take in the word of God like any other soul.

For so long, the black church has been one of the safest places for blacks in an otherwise antagonistic culture. I say safest because I know many will rightly challenge me and point out the numerous ways that the black church has harmed individuals on its own. I acknowledge that, and like any institution with people in it, the black church is not perfect. Nevertheless, I am and will always be a fierce defender of the black church and its contributions to not only black America but the United States as a whole. It was the black church that opened its doors to travelers on the Underground Railroad. It was the black church that offered a platform for the preaching of hope to a people who were subjugated under the strong arm of chattel slavery. It was the black church that called people to action during the oppression of Reconstruction and the lynching of Jim Crow. This was the institution that provided the greatest leaders of the civil rights movement. Here, in 2015, was a black church, with doors open, led by a charismatic and community-focused pastor, only to have one of those welcomed visitors turn his rage against the inviting community.

The funeral of Pinckney demonstrated so much of what I've already written about: the emotional intensity of black death practices, as well as the celebration and pageantry. Above all, Pinckney's funeral at the College of Charleston's TD Arena demonstrated black preaching. I already know that a host of my colleagues are going to disagree strongly with that last sentence, but there is no doubt in my mind that Obama's eulogy of Rev. Pinckney demonstrated a majority of the characteristics of what homilists study in the academy as black preaching. Even though as I have described, Obama's relationship with the black church has never been a highlight of his leadership, I see no difference between what Obama did on that day and what Frederick Douglass, Cornel West, Michael Eric Dyson and others have done under the guise of preaching. Pinckney's funeral was a strange convergence of the princely and the priestly. In the readily available video of the event, one can see the entire episcopacy of the AME church behind Obama fully vested, making it hard to distinguish the actual setting from a real church.

But I will take a more systematic approach to what Obama did to demonstrate the extent to which his "preaching moment" transcended the traditional functions of prince and priest. Firstly, let's acknowledge that Obama began his remarks by "giving all praise and honor to God."[23] Those who are familiar with black sermons know that in the traditional black church setting the sermon begins with introductory remarks that address the House and give honor to various people. Such remarks allow the speaker to both acclimate his or herself and to also show deference to those of perceived importance. Henry A. Mitchell described this necessary aspect of black preaching saying that guest preachers (as Obama would've been that day) "are also required to give due respect to God and to all of the real and imaginary dignitaries on the platform."[24] As he continued his remarks, Obama went on to acknowledge the biblical call to "hope, to persevere and have faith in things not seen," a direct reference to Hebrews 11:1. Throughout the eulogy Obama invoked terms like *anointed, God's word, forsake*, to name a few. Such biblical language was fitting for the deceased preacher and also fitting for the moment, which although not in a church building was in the middle of a worship service.

It was in the recognition that the tragedy hit at the heart of the black church that Obama used his remarks to state some historical truths about the black church:

Our pain cuts that much deeper because it happened in a church. The church is and always has been the center of African American life . . . [applause] . . . a place to call our own in a too-often hostile world, a sanctuary from so many hardships. Over the course of centuries, black churches served as hush harbors, where slaves could worship in safety, praise houses, where their free descendants could gather and shout "Hallelujah . . ." [applause] . . . rest stops for the weary along the Underground Railroad, bunkers for the foot soldiers of the civil rights movement. They have been and continue to be community centers, where we organize for jobs and justice, places of scholarship and network, places where children are loved and fed and kept out of harm's way and told that they are beautiful and smart and taught that they matter. [applause] That's what happens in church. That's what the black church means—our beating heart, the place where our dignity as a people is inviolate. There's no better example of this tradition than Mother Emanuel, a church . . . [applause] . . . a church built by blacks seeking liberty, burned to the ground because its founders sought to end slavery only to rise up again, a phoenix from these ashes. [applause] When there were laws banning all-black church gatherers, services happened here anyway in defiance of unjust laws. When there was a righteous movement to dismantle Jim Crow, Dr. Martin Luther King Jr. preached from its pulpit, and marches began from its steps. A sacred place, this church, not just for blacks, not just for Christians but for every American who cares about the steady expansion . . . [applause] . . . of human rights and human dignity in this country, a foundation stone for liberty and justice for all. That's what the church meant. [applause][25]

Listening to Obama, one unfamiliar with the black church should've come away with a solid understanding of its place in America. Although he spoke in the past tense, using the term *meant*, Obama could've easily said, "That's what the church *means*," because all of the things he mentioned are still relevant.

The theme of Obama's eulogy (sermon) was *grace*. For reference, an informal definition of *grace* that we use in the church is "unmerited favor." Grace described in such a way speaks to human limitations. As empowered as humans are to plant and build and reap and sow, there are some things we simply can't accomplish on our own, and thus we need grace. Without grace we can't look beyond our own prejudices. Without grace we're bound by our own wants and desires. Without grace we're incapable of properly stewarding this creation God has given us charge over. That's why I can appreciate the more formal definition of grace: "unmerited divine assistance given to humans for their regeneration or sanctification."[26] Certainly divine assistance (God's intervention) is cause for celebration. Human limitations don't end up winning, because grace steps in and fills the gap. Utilizing the refrain of grace, Obama ended his eulogy the way every black sermon is supposed to end, in celebration. Mitchell confirms this, writing, "No matter how misused by some or criticized by others, the celebration at its best is the goal to which all of the black sermon is moving."[27] The celebratory nature of the close is evident by the singing and applause that accompanied the words.

If George W. Bush's transcendent presidential moment was his bullhorn speech at Ground Zero, for black America, Barack Obama's was spontaneously singing the first verse of "Amazing Grace" at Pinckney's funeral. So much history and so much emotion converged at that moment. The prince did what the priest is typically tasked with, pointing the people toward the God of grace. As powerful as Obama's sixty-four seconds of singing were (emphasized below with italics), even more powerful for me were the thirteen seconds of silence before he started singing. To this day I haven't been able to discern whether he was overcome with emotion, debating whether or not to sing, or just pensive in the midst of a weighty moment. Whatever the cause for that pause, for me, it remains one of the highlights of the Obama presidency. The pause, represented by an ellipsis below, proceeded singing, repetition, and dramatic intonation of the voice, each of which is one of the things that typifies the celebratory close of a black sermon. It also helped that Obama was fully accompanied in this moment by a Hammond organ. Obama closed the eulogy with these words:

> Amazing grace, amazing grace. *Amazing grace* . . . (SINGING) [applause] . . . *how sweet the sound that saved a wretch like me. I once was lost, but now I'm found, was blind, but now, I see.* [applause] Clementa Pinckney found that grace . . . [applause] . . . Cynthia Hurd found that grace . . . [applause] . . . Susie Jackson found that grace . . . [applause] . . . Ethel Lance found that grace . . . [applause] . . . DePayne Middleton Doctor found that grace . . . [applause] . . . Tywanza Sanders found that grace . . . [applause] . . . Daniel L. Simmons Sr. found that grace . . . [applause] . . . Sharonda Coleman-Singleton found that grace . . . [applause] . . . Myra Thompson found that grace . . . [applause] . . . through the example of their lives. They've now passed it onto us. May we find ourselves worthy of that precious and extraordinary gift as long as our lives endure. May grace now lead them home. May God continue to shed His Grace on the United States of America.[28]

TWO PRIESTHOODS

The Priest as Prayer Leader

One of the ancient practices of religion, especially the Christian faith, is prayer. Prayer precedes the founding of Christianity, being evident throughout biblical accounts in both the Old and New Testaments. Throughout the Bible, prayer is offered as the central action that occurs before God's intervention in a situation. The story of King Hezekiah of Judah and his illness is one such account. Despite receiving a prognosis of death, Hezekiah saw this part of his life story end with an extension of life. In between the death prognosis and the life extension was a powerful moment of prayer in which Hezekiah testified to God. Hezekiah's prayer differed from many prayers throughout the Bible in that it consisted almost exclusively of petition, with little praise to God. I've pivoted to Hezekiah's story because, like Obama at Clementa Pinckney's funeral, Hezekiah displayed a vacillation between the princely and the priestly. Of course, such vacillation is not uncommon in the Old Testament, as there was a much closer connection between the work of princes and the worship of priests. More specifically, the narrative of Hezekiah suggests that there is a connection between our life's testimony and God's response to our petitioning in prayer. If the suggestion is a fact, it indicts much of the American priesthood, not because they are involved in illicit activities or promoting vice, but because their life's testimony speaks to attitudes and actions that don't align with the God of justice we read about in the Bible.

This particular story of King Hezekiah appears in both Isaiah and 2 Kings, with the former being a more succinct account and the latter being more extensive.[1] Several verses of 2 Chronicles also mention Hezekiah's illness, but only briefly. One is hard-pressed to find contradictions between the two primary accounts. When the Isaiah account begins, readers are introduced to Hezekiah, the king of Judah, and they are told that Hezekiah did that which was "right in the sight of the Lord."[2] It is written that Hezekiah trusted in the Lord more than any of his contemporaries or those who ruled before him. Most importantly for purposes of the narrative, we are told in 2 Kings that Hezekiah kept the commandments of the Lord, and we are led to believe that the entire nation was blessed because of Hezekiah's faithfulness to God's commandments. In 2 Kings Hezekiah's righteousness is compared to that of King David. (This comparison, like many of the references to David in the books of the Kings, exalts David's successes as a leader while omitting his personal failures.)[3]

Second Kings also tells of societal wickedness. According to the story, the Hebrews had been burning incense and worshipping a serpentine idol they called Nehushtan, but King Hezekiah recognized that the idol had no place among God's chosen people.[4] Hezekiah is credited with destroying the idol, out of reverence for God. In the 2 Kings account, King Hezekiah is also portrayed as victorious against the enemies of Judah. The thematic lesson seems to be that the righteous living and professional execution of the prince (in this case, Hezekiah) resulted in not only his personal successes, but the successes of the nation. Nevertheless, as a human king, Hezekiah had a human body, and like all humans, he was forced to face death. For Hezekiah, the prognosis was one of his impending demise, but for any human it represents the arrival of difficult or defeating news.

Both 2 Kings 20 and Isaiah 38 describe in detail how the prophet Isaiah appeared before Hezekiah and instructed him, "Set your house in order, for you shall die; you shall not recover."[5] By itself, the pronouncement of death was far from extraordinary, since all humans are expected to both be born and eventually die. Honestly, when you think about it, the pronouncement lacked many details. Even though the prognosis was that Hezekiah would die and "not recover," no time frame was given for when exactly the king would die. The most we are given is an indication that Hezekiah's impending death was to be caused by sickness, with no explanation for the type of sickness or affliction. Any attempt to exegete the text must consider the lack of specifics relating to the time frame for the pronouncement to come to pass. "You shall die; you shall not recover" is not a bold pronouncement, for again, as saddening as it may be to think about, *all* humans have an appointment with death. A more intriguing part of the text is not the message from the prophet, but the subsequent actions of the one who receives the prophecy. The text indicates that after receiving the prophecy, Hezekiah turns his face to the nearest wall and prays.

Prayer is often presented as a conversation, individuals communicating with God, and God communicating with individuals. One element of prayer that shows up consistently is an *acknowledgment* of who God is. Elsewhere in the Bible, as the prophet Nehemiah began to pray for his people, he began his prayer by acknowledging God's greatness, stating, "O Lord God of heaven, the great and awesome God."[6] Another element that is common in prayer is *praise*. Later in his prayer, Nehemiah glorified God, if ever so briefly, by stating, "O Lord, let your ear be attentive to the prayer of your servant, and to the prayer of your servants *who delight in revering your name*."[7] Expressing the desire to *revere* God's name is just one form of praise. In doing so Nehemiah was giving adoration to God. Often, one can find a prayer giving thanks and praise prior to entering a third element, *petition*, or making requests.

The petition aspect of prayer is arguably the one that people think about most. To petition is to ask for things. Nowhere in Hezekiah's story do we find Hezekiah acknowledging God's sovereignty other than maybe when he called God by his name, Yehovah. Neither do we find in the text detail of the ways in which Hezekiah gave praise to God in his prayer. We are simply told that Hezekiah petitioned God, and we are told the nature of that petition. Yet upon examination, Hezekiah's more informal prayer appears to be like so many of the prayers of desperation that are uttered on a regular basis. In moments of crisis and extreme need, formalities are dispensed with, and individuals simply pour out to God expressions from their heart. In some instances, those expressions are raw, uncensored, and unbridled, but in almost all instances they effectively communicate the essence of an immediate need.

Another way to examine Hezekiah's prayer is in the greater context of his life, already described. It is not unreasonable to view Hezekiah's life of righteousness and reign of righteousness as a living testimony to his acknowledgment and praise of God. If that were the case, he would have been approaching God with his petition having already expressed (via the actions of his life) his acknowledgment of who God was, and gratitude for what God had done. Another lesson for us is that if we are to ever be in a position of desperation with God—which most of us will at some point or another be in—it is best to be in that position having already demonstrated via our lives that we acknowledge who God is and are grateful for what he has done. How much better it would be, when in a life-or-death situation, lacking time to bow knees or close eyes and be eloquent, to know with certainty that in the few fleeting moments in which we must pray, God will hear us.

One final consideration is the varying degrees of effectiveness of prayers. We are told of several prayer accounts in the Bible that end in the desired results of the prayer. In the 2nd chapter of 1 Samuel, a woman by the name of Hannah prays to God to have a child, and she promises that if her request is granted, she'll give that child back to God. In the 3rd chapter of 1 Kings, King Solomon is given the opportunity to ask God for anything he wants. Solomon chooses to ask God for wisdom so he can perform his job more effectively. Each of those instances is a story in which the prayer request was answered and demonstrates some of the things that may lead to effective prayer. In Hannah's case, she was willing to make a sacrifice, even a bargain some might say, to have her prayer answered. In Solomon's story, he was willing to forsake many earthly pleasures or material things to have that which could aide him in his God-given assignment. As one assesses Hezekiah's story, we find him also praying an effective prayer. The question is, what was it that distinguished his prayer from others' and caused it to be effective in petitioning God for intervention?

According to the narrative, Hezekiah both prayed and cried, but his first action was to pray. There is much significance here, because in Isaiah 38:2, after receiving the horrible report from the prophet, Hezekiah *immediately* turned his face to the wall and petitioned God. I think we can discern a lot from Hezekiah's first actions. First responses to a crisis speak volumes about who or what someone trusts. In modern times, many are likely to call some sort of a first responder if a crisis arises that threatens safety. For better or for worse, there is near-universal trust in America that when someone dials 9-1-1 a dispatcher *will* answer and some sort of first responder *will* come. Hezekiah's response was to immediately petition God, and that indicated a trust in God. His prayer preceded his expression of grief, which was manifested in tears.

Historically in the black church there is a saying that "prayer changes things," but throughout the Bible we are admonished that not all prayers have the same level of effectiveness. In the Psalms we read, "If I had cherished iniquity in my heart, the Lord would not have listened."[8] In the New Testament epistle of James, we read, "Therefore confess your sins to one another, and pray for one another, so that you may be healed. The prayer of the *righteous* is powerful and effective."[9] James's letter suggests that the righteousness of the one praying makes the prayer more likely to be answered. One final and chilling statement regarding the effectiveness of communication with God is found in the wisdom book of Proverbs. The message to the people is, "Because I have called and you refused . . . and because you have ignored all my counsel . . . I also will laugh at your calamity; I will mock when panic strikes you . . ."[10] That verse appears to imply that it is futile to suddenly seek God's assistance after continuing in unrighteousness and ignoring God's righteousness.

Hezekiah's prayer reflected the attitude of the exemplar described in the 5th chapter of James. As has already been stated, Hezekiah is described as one who did right in God's sight. This appears to have had much bearing on the nature of his prayer, for after he turned his face to the wall and prayed, he testified back to God about himself. Hezekiah stated, "Remember now, O Lord, I implore you, how I have walked before you in faithfulness with a whole heart, and have done what is good in your sight."[11] It was not until after Hezekiah asked God to remember, that he wept. I've always drawn significance out of that for several reasons, the most important of which is that it shows the extent of Hezekiah's trust in God. His very first reaction was to speak to the one that he believed had the power to intervene on his behalf. This is another testament to the righteousness of this king. Even before his very understandable human emotion of grief and despair set in, the king understood that his best recourse, having been presented with certain death— "you shall not recover"—was to talk to his God.

We would be left to question if one's testimony to God in prayer mattered, except for the fact that the next few verses establish that God heard Hezekiah's prayer and then took several actions because of what was heard. The word came to Isaiah that he was to return to Hezekiah and let him know that God was going to add fifteen years to his life. The additional fifteen years might have been by chance, but the text indicates otherwise, because God's message was, "I have heard your prayer, I have seen your tears."[12] While Hezekiah's tears were an expression of his human reaction to detrimental news, his testimony reminding God of his faithfulness was an expression of his spiritual fortitude. The tears would have been of no good if there was unrighteousness behind them. Even the ancient historian Josephus emphasized Hezekiah's piety in his accounts of the king, choosing to omit other narratives, including an account in 2 Chronicles 32 that questions Hezekiah's righteousness.[13]

Unfortunately, the biblical accounts of Hezekiah portray him as making less than righteous decisions after the extension of his life is granted, but there is no doubt that the book of Isiah leads us to believe that the righteousness of Hezekiah preceding his illness provided him with good standing before God. With good standing, Hezekiah was able to petition God in earnest, largely omitting praise, and subsequently see the granting of his request in the form of an extension of his life. Hezekiah was able to testify in prayer, leading to an effective petition.

The Curious Case of Franklin Graham

I've offered a brief biblical survey of prayer to, as I've attempted to do throughout this book, contrast what the Bible presents to the contemporary actions and words of some who claim to minister from that Bible. In recent years, there have been plenty of examples of prayer that have disturbed me, but maybe none as much as a particularly offensive Day of Prayer. Few last names are more connected to American Christian leadership than Graham. Through a combination of factors, reverend Franklin Graham has become one of the most prominent evangelical leaders in the nation. The son of American evangelist Billy Graham, Rev. Graham has garnered the respect of many in the evangelical community and is now considered one of that population's chief spokespersons.

In late May 2019, Rev. Graham called on the nation to engage in a special day of prayer. Nothing too strange about that. America has held national days of prayer and fasting for centuries. According to Forrest Church, even John Adams wrote national fast day proclamations, and apparently Adams utilized the "language of Puritan covenant theology" to do so.[14] Despite the establishment and separation clauses of the Constitution protecting religious liberty and protecting against religious tyranny, public calls for prayer have long been viewed as appropriate for our country. Rev. Graham's call for prayer, however, spoke to a more questionable agenda. His was a request for the nation to pray for Donald Trump, "that God would protect, strengthen, embolden, and direct him." Pause.

Like national prayer days, there is nothing unusual about a specific call to pray for a president. If one is searching for a biblical justification, the Bible is replete with scriptures that urge individuals to pray for those who occupy various positions of authority. In the first letter to Timothy, instructions are given concerning prayer, which begin by urging Timothy to pray for *everyone*. The instructions further call on

Timothy to specifically pray "for kings and all who are in high positions."[15] In the 2nd chapter of 1 Peter, citizens are instructed to submit to governing authorities and to honor those who rule—essentially an instruction to follow what we know today as the rule of law. The same scriptures also admonish those in authority to lead in a just manner. In the Psalms, leaders are instructed to "serve the Lord with reverent awe and worshipful fear."[16] Such a directive suggests that as much as citizens are supposed to honor and pray for the ones in authority, the ones in authority have a responsibility to handle their responsibilities justly.

Other canonical passages identify governmental leaders who seemingly understand that they need God's intervention to be successful in guiding national affairs. These examples include Joseph in his tenure as prime minister of Egypt, David and his leadership of national worship, Solomon's dedication of the national temple, and the Queen of Sheba's acknowledgment of Solomon's favor with his God. If a biblical example is to be found, it is one of both citizens and leaders having a role to play in holding the government to a standard of just leadership. Given then what the scriptures say about praying for leaders, we should emphatically call out as suspect any major Christian figure who chooses to pray for one president after cursing the previous one.

On February 21, 2012, Rev. Graham, on national TV, couldn't state conclusively that he believed then-president Barack Obama was a Christian, despite Obama affirming his Christianity on many prior occasions. To his credit, Rev. Graham later apologized for his statements, but that instance was just one in a pattern of instances in which Rev. Graham had shown an unfortunate disregard for the faith of the former president. In 2016 he accused President Obama of leading an "all-out war on religious liberty." At the time Rev. Graham based that belief on Obama's support for things like same-sex marriage and abortion rights, but at no time did he ever call a national prayer for said president.

In the same series of 2016 statements, Rev. Graham suggested that President Obama, who has only been married one time and has two children by the same woman, was somehow helping to "lead the fight to promote ungodly sexual behavior." Today it is clear that such statements are laden with hypocrisy given that President Trump has been married three times and has regularly used crass sexual language to describe females, particularly female political opponents.

Sunday, June 2, 2019, was Rev. Graham's Special Day of Prayer for President Trump. The special page on the Billy Graham Evangelistic Association website advertising the event displayed Ephesians 6:12: "For we do not wrestle against flesh and blood, but against principalities." The way it appeared, it was almost as if those who disagree with or are working against the political objectives of this president are somehow agents of *rulers of darkness* or *spiritual wickedness*. Interestingly enough, after searching, I couldn't find anywhere where Rev. Graham prayed for the president to forsake the wickedness of equivocating white nationalists and "fine people."[17] There was no call to pray for President Trump to enact policies that could stem the tide of more than 33,000 Americans dying due to guns each year, or to stop the harmful caging of immigrant children or cease patterns of environmental negligence.

Such hypocrisy has been stamped onto the veneer of much of American evangelical Christianity. Not only does this hypocrisy cry out for prophetic challenge, but it also cries out for more education on the part of its chief spokespersons. With such education, evangelical leaders like Rev. Graham may have encountered such passages like the one in which Daniel Guder and his colleagues suggest that if we are to "seek first the reign of God and God's justice," we should focus our public actions "away from imposing our moral will onto the social fabric and toward giving tangible experience of the reign of God that intrudes as an alternative to the public principles and loyalties."[18] Imposition—either in word or in deed—is easy, giving tangible expression is much more difficult and implies commitment and sacrifice. It is much more convenient to attempt to force society into the narrow box of one's interpretation of morality than it is to display those acts that most characterize what godly morality should look and feel like: clothing the naked, feeding the hungry, displaying mercy, embracing the other, etc.

As such, what was most troubling about Graham's call for prayer was not that it was a call for prayer, but the hypocritical nature of the call. Like budgets in the business world, prayer lists in the faith world reveal priorities. After September 11, 2001, the special National Day of Prayer showed the world just how important the safety and security of the nation were to the American people. Even more than that, it showed how important it was for Americans to heal from the shock of learning that we were probably more vulnerable than we thought. Prayer services during presidential inaugural festivities reveal our desire for the executive leadership to be led into good decision-making, thus helping to ensure the prosperity of the country.

If prayer lists reveal our priorities, we should be concerned when certain things are absent from the list. When the hypocrisy that has unfortunately characterized too much of mainstream Christianity spills over into such a basic spiritual practice as prayer, we should be extremely concerned. Never once did Franklin Graham call a day of prayer for President Barack Obama, quite the opposite. Rev. Graham boldly suggested that Obama was an instrument of evil forces. It's not clear why Rev. Graham and others have displayed such hypocrisy, but we should have our suspicions. Could it be that the standards for a white Christian President are different than those for a black Christian President? Or maybe it really is just about politics, and the current president has afforded Rev. Graham and his contemporaries more access than the former one. Only Rev. Graham and his evangelical friends know the answer. What we do know, if the biblical accounts are to be believed, is that prayer is always in order, and not all prayers are the same. *Prayerfully*, Rev. Graham, and indeed all of us, can check our hypocrisy when it comes to the things we pray about.

Betsy DeVos and the Priesthood

The effects of what I like to call the dominant priesthood go beyond days of prayer; they now reach the highest levels of government. A prominent example is in secretary of education Betsy DeVos, whose Senate confirmation vote for a cabinet post is still the only one in US history to require the vice president to break a tie. DeVos demonstrated that she was not qualified for the position, but political forces confirmed her nonetheless. For the purposes of this writing, I want to highlight the role of religion in her work.

Since her confirmation on February 7, 2017, the public has been treated to her repeated displays of disdain for public education. Even strong public education advocates like myself should acknowledge that the faith community has a role to play in education. Much good can come out of local institutions of faith partnering with local schools. Sometimes such partnerships can take the form of volunteer exchanges for things like tutoring and other afterschool programs, or even something as simple as school supply drives at the end of the summer. Also, for years parochial schools have offered an alternative to public schools, even if not always an equally accessible alternative. For some, religious schools offer families the opportunity to educate their children in a more faith-focused environment. Families that choose this option accept that they are waiving their right to what their tax dollars pay for and choosing to have their children educated in a school that they deem more appropriate for their family's needs.

That choice continues to provide some diversity and opportunity in the American education system. Unfortunately, "choice" for Mrs. DeVos means support for religious schools at the expense of public ones. In 2013 she stated, "Traditional public schools are not succeeding. In fact, let's be clear, in many cases, they are failing."[19] She went on to state, "That's helped people become more open to what were once considered really radical reforms . . . vouchers, tax credits, and education savings accounts." There are many of us who see those particular reforms for what they are—an overt way to destroy public education. Unlike the secretary, some of us in education still believe that public education is one of the bedrocks of American society and that that particular bedrock is best left protected from the intrusion of, among other things, religion. Regarding vouchers for religious schools, the first amendment ensures that American citizens (and their schools and tax dollars) are protected from government-endorsed religion. Similarly, that same amendment ensures that citizens can freely exercise their own faith, and in some cases that free exercise is manifest in the form of a religious education—paid for by the individual, not the community.

It can be tempting to cosign Mrs. DeVos's beliefs, especially when they're presented in the generic terms education reformers use. In remarks on November 30, 2017, at the tenth anniversary summit of Jeb Bush's Foundation for Excellence in Education (now ExcelinEd), the secretary claimed that she and the other reformers present shared the common goal of equipping "every child in America with the education necessary to achieve his or her God-given potential."[20] After three years in office and years of support for mediocre education reforms, it's clear that for Mrs. DeVos, the pathway to God-given potential is the denigration of teachers, the diversion of funds to religious-affiliated institutions, and the shuttering of traditional public schools.

It's as if for Mrs. DeVos, America is somehow still in Cold War 1983, and *A Nation at Risk* is ostensibly a more hallowed tome than the very US Constitution. That Reagan-era report claimed that American education was "being eroded by a rising tide of mediocrity."[21] Yet it's amazing that for all of our supposed mediocrity, our nation and education systems remain bastions of innovation and ingenuity. In her ExcelinEd remarks, Mrs. DeVos cited the recent Programme for International Student Assessment (PISA) results, which she claimed "shows America stuck in the middle of our international peers." The truth is America has never performed well on these assessments, and they shouldn't be our measuring stick for success. America is not Estonia, nor is it Finland. It's quite ironic that Mrs. DeVos wants us to be more like Finland, all while supporting policies that are opposite of the things Finland does to support education. Finnish public schools are full-service, providing daily hot meals and health and dental services. Finnish public schools ensure that students have access to guidance and psychological services. None of those services can be provided when funds are taken away from public schools for religious schools or otherwise.

I've written about my concerns with the DeVoses for some time. It is one thing when someone represents bad policy views of the dominant Christian culture, but it is another thing when those individuals have immense resources with which to carry out their policy objectives. DeVos has never been an expert on education, but she and her family are wealthy. Wealth alone is not a bad thing; it can be a good thing, especially when used in the right ways. Unfortunately, for at least the last two decades, DeVos and her family have used their wealth to push an agenda that is based on evangelical tripe. Just one compelling piece of evidence of this is part of the transcript from remarks DeVos and her husband gave at a 2001 gathering of wealthy Christians called "The Gathering." I've included part of the interview here to help readers better understand the way DeVos's Christianity influences her policy positions [emphasis mine].

> Dick DeVos: If we look at the policy issue, I would just encourage those who are interested in this to look at public schools because we use the word public schools and what we're really talking about is the content of public education. And so, what I try to explain to people in the midst of our campaign was to challenge folks and say let's look past your own history. Look at what is the objective of public education and what should it be within our community. It ought to be in our community offering every child, no matter where they come from, no matter what their background economic or otherwise, the very best educational opportunity we can provide. Isn't that what public education is, as opposed to exclusive education or discriminating education? This is about allowing every child that desires an education to achieve the highest level of education. Now let's not confuse that very laudable concept with the way we currently apply it in America, which is forcing people to operate within what are in most cases *government-run schools*. That is an execution that is an attempt to deliver this higher promise. The real promise that has been one of the great things for America has been access to quality education, it hasn't been the way we've delivered it.

> Interviewer: **But wouldn't it have been easier to simply fund Christian private schools and be done with it? Just build up great Christian private schools**.

Dick: Absolutely.

Betsy DeVos: But the fact is . . . there are not enough phil-
anthropic dollars in America to fund what is currently the
need in education. We could give every single penny we
have, everybody in this room could give every single penny
that they have and it wouldn't begin to touch what is currently spent on education every year in this country. And
what is, in many cases, not efficiently spent or not well spent.
So our desire, and this is another thing that we learned a
couple of years ago, we went on a trip to Israel with a mar-
velous teacher who talked about the geography in Israel,
where the coastal plain where the **pagans** lived, the **Israelites** lived in the foothills and the crescent in between was
called the Shfela. And he really challenged all of us on that
trip to be active in the Shfela. The Shfela where the cultures
meet, and that has been something that has been really impactful for both Dick and me, is to continue to think about
where we can be the most effective or make the most impact
in the culture in which we live today. **And so, our desire
is to be in that Shfela, to confront the culture in
which we all live today in ways which will continue
to help advance God's kingdom. Not to stay in our
own little safe territory.**

Dick: It would have been a lot easier and a lot less controversial to just go fund the small number of private schools
that possibly we could have funded. But what about those
kids in the urban community in Detroit that wouldn't have
the ability to access, and what are we going to do to drive
for better performance across all of our education? **It was
really a systemic view that we looked at, and it was
working within that Shfela to allow for our Christian worldview to be, our Christian world view
which for us comes from a Calvinist tradition,**

which is to be very much a part of the world and to provide for greater opportunity, an expanded opportunity some day for all parents to be able to educate their children in a school that reflects their worldview and not each day sending their child to a school that may be reflecting a world view quite antithetical, which unfortunately is the case in some places to the world view that they hold with their family.

Interviewer: Some people, maybe even in this room, would say why waste your dollars on non-Christian things? Just support Christian things. Why get involved in politics? Why get involved in public education? Why do those things? I mean if you are really going to be a Christian, just fund Christian things. You've chosen not to do that.

Betsy: Well I think it goes back to what I just mentioned, the concept of really being active in the Shfela of our culture. To impact our culture in ways that are not the traditional funding the Christian organization route, **but that really may have greater kingdom gain in the long run by changing the way we approach things. In this case the system of education in the country**.

Dick: Let me just take you to a quick trip to an archaeological dig in the Shfela in Israel. And the archaeologists in this particular community, which was between where the pagans lived on the coastal plain where the Philistines lived and where the Israelites lived up in the mountains. And as the archaeologists went down, they found that there were, they found in various food storage areas, they found varying layers as the years went by where some layers were completely devoid of pig bones and pig remains. And other layers there were pig remains integrated throughout that community. If you're familiar with Jewish tradition, obviously

pigs are not kosher, those were not acceptable for eating. So
. . . if in fact the Jewish people were influencing that community, the pig bones were gone. They were out of there,
and so there were periods of time when the Jewish community was influencing that town, and there were times when
obviously . . . their influence wasn't being felt at all; the pig
bones were right back in. So the question that we continue
to challenge with is to say we could run away and just go
back up into the hills and live very safely and very comfort-
ably, or are we going to exist on the Shfela and try to impact
the view of the community around us with the ideas that we
believe are more powerful ideas of a better way to live one's
life and a more meaningful and a more rewarding way to
live one's life as a Christian than to just run away in the hills
and allow the world to spin around us? And we keep going
back and saying, our job is to figure out, in a contemporary
context, how do we get the pig bones out of our culture?[22]

For a moment, I want to take the DeVos concept of Shfela and
deal with it more thoroughly. The DeVoses have identified public education as one point of Shfela, one point where cultures meet. They
reference ideas and impact, but never once do they use the word *impose*
or the term *imposition,* which more accurately reflects what they've
been trying to do. Sure, no one can blame wealthy people for using
their money and influence to try to make things happen— that happens all of the time. One could probably say that our world exists the
way it does now because over time philanthropists and others with
vested interests have appropriated resources for various things that
they care about. It also seems from their remarks that the DeVoses
identify themselves as instruments of the priestly function. It just seems
to me that there are better ways to go about advancing God's Kingdom. Does one having a good public education mean that it has to
occur under the guise of religious education? Of course not, but when

the objective is to proselytize as opposed to just educate, we find people like the DeVoses throwing money around and having outsized success achieving their objectives.

Part III
The Prophets

FINDING THE ALTERNATIVE

Both princes and priests have to contend with the weight of their mandates. However, no mandate is weightier than the one borne by a prophet. In his famous work *The Prophetic Imagination*, Walter Brueggemann challenged the then-prevailing notions of prophetic work. In so doing, he gave us a framework that is applicable to the prophetic calling in every context. Many of Brueggemann's arguments in *Prophetic Imagination* concerned the role of prophets in speaking to society's outlook, as evidenced by the hypothesis of the book in which he suggests that prophets are supposed to "nurture, nourish, and evoke a consciousness and perception alternative to the consciousness and perception of the dominant culture."[1] The prophets are charged with speaking to the challenges in society. It is true that a prince protects people against challenges and has to work to find solutions for those challenges. It is also true that priests are charged with ministering to the people in the midst of the challenges, elevating worship in spite of the challenges, and bearing the burdens of the people *through* the challenges. The prophets, on the other hand, must contend with the very forces of evil, sometimes manifested in the form of the princes and the priests themselves. For that reason alone, the prophets have the most difficult obligation of the three. It is theirs to speak truth to others in power. Inherent in the office of prince is governing power. Inherent in the office of priest is religious and moral power. The prophet's power, however, is not derived from statute, but rather from the calling itself. Make no mistake:

the prophets have some power of their own, but the power they have is to be used to confront power held by others. Needless to say, that is not an easy assignment. It shouldn't surprise us then that true prophets are rare.

The Prophetic Example

Throughout the Bible's prophetic books, God's anger is vividly described, and the actions resulting from that anger are clearly detailed. The prophets, speaking as the oracles of God, provide for the people God's heart concerning their hearts. The prophets relay God's feelings regarding the people's attitudes and their lack of alignment with the covenant God has made with them. The book of Jeremiah details as much, displaying Israel's progressive forsaking of God and the lack of reliance upon the same. The obvious result was the kindling of God's anger. The prophetic work of Hosea also lays out God's charge against Israel, portraying the nation as an unfaithful spouse. In Micah, the Lord established a case against Israel, citing their false prophets and corrupt leaders. Yet in the midst of all of the pronouncements of destruction, God's love for God's people manifests in the form of promises of restoration, provided the people are willing to embrace righteousness and live in accordance with the covenant God had provided them.

In the book of Jeremiah, after reading of Jeremiah's call in his youth, we read a pronouncement of destruction upon Israel. The word comes that judgments will be uttered because God has been forsaken and other gods have been worshiped.[2] This verse typifies many in the prophets, as pronouncements of destruction are explained. It is hard to find a place where a prophet prophesies destruction and no charge is presented against the recipient of the destruction. In one powerful set of verses, Jeremiah states that the prophets are prophesying lies, the priests are acting of their own accord, and worst of all, the people love this condition.[3] At the end of verse 31 is an ominous rhetorical question, "But what will you do when the end comes?" That rhetorical question says a lot about how God feels about Israel in that state. A few chapters later in chapter 7, Jeremiah records God listing some of the evil that the people have done, including defiling the temple with idols and sacrificing children. While the specific form of offense is varied, all the offenses of the people amount to an unfaithfulness to God. Ultimately, the offenses that Jeremiah lists demonstrate that God's anger is most kindled by the people's lack of faithfulness to their covenant.

Hosea also details God's anger and does so through the analogy of an unfaithful spouse. Hosea himself must deal with an unfaithful wife, and conceivably this is so that the prophet can fully understand the grievances God has against the nation he has been commissioned to prophesy to. God tells Hosea, "Go, love a woman who has a lover and is an adulteress, just as the Lord loves the people of Israel, though they turn to other gods."[4] God's accusations against Israel as presented in Hosea include swearing, lying, and murder, as well as the rejection of knowledge, and idolatry. Yet the terms *whoredom* and *adultery* are used, leading one to believe that again, God's greatest grievance is that the people have been unfaithful to something, in this case they have been unfaithful to God. The word then comes that because of this unfaithfulness, judgment is coming their way.

A final example of cause for God's violent judgment is found in Micah. It is declared in this book that "the Lord has a case against his people . . . a charge against Israel."[5] The guilt of Israel is that they are dishonest and those with power (particularly the rich) are violent and deceitful. Because of this unfaithfulness, we are presented with violent imagery to describe God's destruction of the transgressing people.

Earlier in the book of Micah we read of the manifestations of judgment, including broken idols, burned temples, weeping and nakedness, all of which amount to suffering. Further, false prophets seem to wield tremendous influence over what happens in the land. These things kindle God's anger and lead to the pronounced destruction.

Still, during the destruction that is pronounced, the mercy of God is present. Even while laying out the case for the evil that has been and is being committed, deliverance is promised for the people. In the 7th chapter of Micah it is declared that God will allow Israel to rise. The prophet writes that Israel will "bear the Lord's wrath until he pleads my case . . . He will bring me out into the light."[6] The acknowledgment of sin and the willingness to bear whatever it is that God has for the people demonstrates the level of humility that God seems to be looking for before he can send deliverance. While each of the passages discussed demonstrate that sin has very real consequences, this 7th chapter of Micah is just one example of how the people's sincere desire to forsake unrighteousness (repentance) can lead to restoration and deliverance. It is the task of the prophet to call the people to such an aspiration.

Humpty Dumpty

One examination that can help us see the contemporary relevance of the prophetic discussion is that of walls. Walls are used for so many different purposes. According to the famous English nursery rhyme, Humpty Dumpty sat on one and eventually fell off of it. Most of us are familiar with Mr. Dumpty's tragic end. As a child that cute little rhyme entertained me, but at this point in life the preacher in me who sees symbolism almost everywhere can't help but see some parallels between Humpty Dumpty and the current president of the United States. Mr. Trump rose to power in large part staking his claims on an unrealistic wall. If you ask many of us, Mr. Trump has had more than one or two falls. He's had myriad falls: moral falls, judgement falls, and leadership falls, just to name a few. As the president of the United States, the most influential leadership position on earth, Mr. Trump has access to the greatest of resources. He can summon the counsel of the most accomplished scholars. At a moment's notice Mr. Trump can assemble a quorum of Fortune 500 business leaders. Yet with all of these figurative horses and all of these figurative men at his disposal, Mr. Trump has yet to display any example of being put together. The truth is, as a leader, he has never been put together. He is, and I am confident that history will view him as, an elected Humpty Dumpty. He and his wall.

I mention walls because walls have been inextricably tied to the presidential narrative of Donald Trump. Some time ago if you asked about the historical significance of walls, many people in the Western world might have mentioned the Berlin Wall which marked the separation between Eastern and Western Germany. Today many millennials best know the wall that's on their Facebook page, where people write and leave them messages, and the symbolism there cannot be ignored because if nothing else walls communicate messages. Too often when we consider walls, we think about them negatively, finding them to cause separation or division, but in reality, walls are important and necessary.

At this very moment, if I look in any direction, I see one of four walls, and they're important because they are both keeping me protected from the weather outside and protecting what I have inside. As much time as I may spend in the gym lifting, and as much as I like to think I can defend myself, I'm honest enough to admit I need some walls. We all do.

Nehemiah's Walls

According to the biblical narrative, in the middle of their history the Israelites were taken away into captivity to a place called Babylon. Eventually they came into favor there, and King Cyrus allowed them to return to their home and begin the process of putting things back together. It was at that time that King Cyrus told the Israelites to focus on their God, which meant rebuilding their destroyed temple. Before they focused on anything else, they needed to restore the place that helped them worship their God because for them, the temple represented God and their relationship with God. For the Israelites the temple was central to their identity as the aspiration was for their identity and their God to be one and the same.

The historical pairing that is the books of Nehemiah and Ezra tells two parts of the same story, of how after their time in captivity the Israelites began the process of rebuilding and putting back together what was destroyed. Over time they worked on the Temple, and despite the obstacles, they were able to complete the temple. But then another young man came on the scene. God had favored this young man, whose name was Nehemiah, and even though Nehemiah had probably never seen Jerusalem with his own eyes, he desired to please his God. Nehemiah was emotionally affected when he learned that the city might be destroyed. He understood that it made no sense to have a beautiful temple if it could not be protected—all because the walls protecting the city were in shambles.

Reading through Nehemiah, one is led to ask several questions: What do you do when your defenses have been destroyed? What do you do when part of your life is together, but there's no sense of security because other parts are chaotic? We all have different needs, but in his groundbreaking work of psychology Abraham Maslow let us know that some needs are universal and they appear in a hierarchy: (1) Biological and physiological needs like air, food, drink, and shelter; (2) Safety needs like protection from the elements, security, order, law, stability, freedom from fear; (3) The need to be loved and feel belonging, including friendship, intimacy, affection, family, friends, and romantic relationships; (4) Esteem needs like a sense of achievement, mastery, independence, status, self-respect, and respect from others; (5) Lastly, self-actualization needs, including the need to realize personal potential and self-fulfillment and seek growth or expanded experiences.[7]

Nehemiah heard about the condition of the walls of Jerusalem and was grieved. As with so many individuals who do extraordinary things, Nehemiah wasn't necessarily a predictable candidate for historical significance. He was just a butler to the ruler, but in consideration of the story it's almost as if he was strategically placed in this service. The story goes that Cyrus noticed Nehemiah's graven countenance. Nehemiah's physical person displayed his anguish. When confronted about it, Nehemiah was finally able to convey, in so many words, that he was troubled by the condition of the wall of security in Jerusalem.

What does one do when there's no sense of protection because their needs aren't being met? There are always options, some of them just and others unjust, some profitable and others destructive. If such individuals are like Nehemiah, they take the positive step of rebuilding the walls, not to separate or divide, not to boast of power or might, but to protect.

Fast-forward and a new king, Artaxerxes, gives Nehemiah permission to return to lead the rebuilding of Jerusalem's walls. Not only was Nehemiah given permission to go back to Jerusalem and rebuild, but Artaxerxes also made him the governor of Jerusalem. It's important to remember that Nehemiah wasn't the priest. The priest's role was to minister to and intercede on behalf of the people—that's why the priest went into the temple to worship. Nehemiah wasn't what we would consider a prophet; the prophet's role was to reveal the will of

God to the people and challenge the leadership and the people. Nehemiah ended up in the position of prince, and as such his role was to protect. How else would one protect except to ensure that the city's walls were sure and its inhabitants secure inside? However, like all princes, Nehemiah faced a set of problems. His problems had names, three to be exact; they were personified by three men named Sanballat, Tobiah, and Geshem.

Priests could effortlessly provide ministry, and princes could protect with ease if only problems didn't arise. The problems are what cause us to need prophets. Prophets are called to problems. They are born for such a time as the one they live in, and they speak to challenges that others are either unwilling or unable to speak to. Nehemiah's problems demonstrate the nature of problems that prophets face. We can exegete even more meaning by looking at the etymology of each of Nehemiah's three primary detractors. The name Sanballat roughly translated means "enemy in secret."[8] The first thing we must consider is that prophets are charged with exposing and combating secret enemies. Of course, not necessarily a secret to them, but they are sometimes tasked with fighting the secret forces that threaten a people, and sometimes the best way to fight a secret is by exposing it. That's why many times in the biblical account the task of the prophet is to "cry loud and spare not." It was theirs to sound a proverbial alarm around issues of national importance. The name Tobiah means "God is good," and hanging above all else that a God-sent prophet has to remember is that God is good. I'm sure that seems fairly commonsense to most readers, but in the midst of a prophetic mandate it's not always the first thing that comes to mind. If it were, we wouldn't find biblical examples of people like Jeremiah hating the mandate they were given. The prophet has to remember that in both mercy and justice, in both law and Gospel, in peace and war, ease and difficulty, simple task and hard one, God is good, and God's goodness supersedes everything else.

Lastly, the name of the third opponent of Israel was Geshem, which means "rain." Unlike the symbolic meaning of the first opponent's name, rain is not secret at all. Rain is the epitome of obvious. As much as it sometimes tries to be silent, rain always makes a noise, if even a soft one. However, for those who are prophetic in nature, they have the ability to see past the obvious inconvenience of rain and discern its greater purpose. Even the most violent of rain fills reservoirs, washes away disease, and nourishes crops. The prophet has to see past inconvenience and see the alternative viewpoint.

Trump's Walls

Nehemiah didn't start out as prince; his righteous motivations made way for him to be appointed to that position. If the example from Nehemiah is to be trusted, the walls that are most needed by nations and princes are not ones created to separate or divide, but ones that are intended to protect. History is brimming with examples of such walls. The greatest example is probably that impressive construction of successive Chinese dynasties that we know as the Great Wall of China. This wall, with sections dating back to the seventh century BC, was designed to protect China from various groups that might have invaded from the north. Due to its scale and impressive construction, the Great Wall of China gets a lot of attention, but make no mistake; it's not the only significant wall built for protection. Other such examples include Iran's Great Wall of Gorgan, which is the world's second-longest wall, as well as the walls built by emperors Aurelian and Probus in Rome. These are examples of constructions that were initiated by leaders to care for and shelter people. They were fortifications that were supposed to keep nations safe. In order to build a wall that keeps a nation safe, a leader needs to have a true understanding of what a nation really is.

If a nation is just a land and the people who occupy it, then build-ing physical barriers to block out invading people is all that's needed. However, if a nation is built on the notion of multiple peoples coming together to enhance one idea of opportunity, a physical wall is likely not enough and might not necessarily be desired at all.

Fast-forward to the modern day, and unlike the impressive leaders who erected the previous structures, America has a leader who on the face of it is crying out for prophetic attention. One of the areas in which a leader can be most dangerous is through their language, either spoken or written (or tweeted). The prophets present both the powers and the people with the language of newness, which means that one can identify the opposite of prophetic action by that which elevates the opposite of newness—oldness. Brueggemann wrote, "It is the aim of every totalitarian effort to stop the language of newness, and we are now learning that where such language stops, we find our humanness diminished."[9] When newness ceases, so too does humanness. It is at the stopping point of newness that we find living human children sep-arated from their parents at America's southern border. It is at this same point that we find national leaders—in the midst of a pan-demic—encouraging individuals to resume large gatherings knowing that the consequence of such gatherings will be the certain spread of disease and eventual death. When one stops at the longitude and lati-tude of this particular place, they find themselves in cities where hatred governs and fears abound. This same hatred has allowed countless Americans to die without ever paying the price for the lynchings they committed and the same fears that took the life of Ahmaud Arbery in February 2020 as he jogged down a residential street, Breonna Taylor in March 2020 as she lay next to her boyfriend minding her own busi-ness, or George Floyd in May 2020 as he was brutalized by the police arresting him.

Donald John Trump has consistently and persistently demonstrated in both word and deed that he is unfit to serve in the role of American prince and is in desperate need of the American prophets. Nehemiah repaired walls. No, he wasn't one of the ones on his knees wielding a trowel or physically doing repair work, but he did display the leadership that was needed to get the job done. When prophets fulfill their mandate, they too help repair walls of protection. America now has a president who wants to build walls of division.

The genesis of President Trump's obsession with a border wall was 2014 when campaign advisors Sam Nunberg and Roger Stone sought a device for Trump to speak about his views on immigration and woo conservative voters.[10] The entire premise of Trump's wall is that America is under attack, not from elements within, but from individuals outside of it. I have no doubt that the hard work of national security officials thwarts plots against national security every day. I accept that there are individuals who want to do our nation harm, but we kid ourselves if we think the threats are coming from migrants at the border. If anything, the threats that some of us are most concerned about are ones right here in America. I'm talking about the dangerous ideologies that radicalize individuals to shoot churches and commit heinous acts against innocent individuals. Such ideologies are promoted with red hats that read "Make America Great Again" (MAGA).

One might consider Langston Hughes a literary and poetic prophet. In 1936 he wrote a prophetic alternative to MAGA in the form of a poem titled "Let America Be America Again." In this poem Hughes wrote:

> Let America be America again
> Let it be the dream it used to be.
> Let it be the pioneer on the plain
> Seeking a home where he himself is free.
> (America never was America to me) . . .

167

O, yes,

I say it plain,

America never was America to me,

America will be! [11]

Those who find no fault in wearing a MAGA hat may be exercising freedom of expression, but they're also exemplifying the staleness of thought that is the antithesis of the prophetic. It is there that Brueggemann says we are co-opted when "we do not believe that there will be newness but only that there will be merely a moving of the pieces into new patterns."[12] The prophetic alternative rejects the language of "Great Again" not only because it is formed from a deficit-minded place, and not only because of the denial of the not-so-great realities of much of our history, but most importantly because of that word *again*. There can be no doubt that parts of America have always been great. We have always been blessed with beautiful acres famously versed as amber waves of grain, purple mountain majesties, and fruited plain![13] We've always had a hardworking people who have toiled ground, leveled mountain, laid track, dug, hulled, welded, wired, tunneled, hammered, soldered, and any other of the million agrarian and industrial verbs that apply to the work of Americans' hands. Similarly, the story of America is one of ingenuity and innovation. The problem is that MAGA neglects to acknowledge the other side of our successes. Kicked off of the fruited plan were millions of native Americans who contrary to popular opinion were on this land first. Many of the millions who performed those verbs I mentioned did so because they had no choice in the matter—as slaves they had no agency in the use of their labor. For every example of ingenuity and innovation, there is at least one example of the same being used to harm, exploit, or kill.

I've already mentioned civil religion in the role of the prince, but we find that civil religion has a prophetic function as well. The prophetic function of civil religion is to keep a nation on the *path* of righteousness.[14] The word *path* is emphasized because the prophet's role is not to place a people somewhere—he or she alone could never do that. The prophet's role is to call a people to a place, and to offer that better place as an alternative to the place at which a people currently is. There is an alternative to MAGA; it's not packaged in an easily-brandable acronym, but it's expressed in the spirit of those who continually challenge—in word and in deed—America to be great. It is at that place, the point of alternative, that we find Johns and Joannas in the wilderness daring us to prepare the way for better. That place is the prophetic, and those who dwell there, and call others to be there, are true prophets.

WHEN JUSTICE IS TURNED BACK

Few texts anywhere lay bare the theme of prophetic justice as much as the book of Isaiah. I have always been surprised at how quotable Isaiah is, but even still I've found myself particularly intrigued by the 59th chapter. In repeated instances throughout that chapter the concept of *justice* has jumped out. More and more I find *justice* is a topic of thought and conversation that popular culture is being forced to acknowledge. There are four verses in particular that I've highlighted in my own Bibles. Each of them deals with justice (emphasis my own):

> v.4 No one brings suit justly,
> no one goes to law honestly;
> they rely on empty pleas, they speak lies,
> conceiving mischief and begetting iniquity.
> v.9 Therefore justice is far from us,
> and righteousness does not reach us;
> we wait for light, and lo! there is darkness;
> and for brightness, but we walk in gloom.
> v.14 Justice is turned back,
> and righteousness stands at a distance;
> for truth stumbles in the public square,
> and uprightness cannot enter.
> v.15 Truth is lacking,
> and whoever turns from evil is despoiled.
> The Lord saw it, and it displeased him
> that there was no justice.[1]

The New Revised Standard Version titles this chapter "Injustice and Oppression to Be Punished," and it is impossible for me to read without thinking about how important the conversation of justice is in 2020. Time and again we think of righteousness in terms of legalism. Despite much scripture that suggests otherwise, many are quick to evaluate their standing with God based on what they did or did not do in terms of ritual or practice. Here, the prophetic scripture is super explicit that in the circumstances outlined in the passage, it is more of a social justice and integrity that is lacking, and the consequence is a fateful separation from truth.

I guess what I'm really getting to is that this 59th chapter of Isaiah is yet another place in scripture where the notion of a Gospel of justice is affirmed. It's another place where the Bible presents God as being on the side of integrity and truth. Clause b of verse 15 states, "The Lord looked and was displeased that there was no justice." If one is to believe that the God they worship is just, then they should also believe that their relationship with God ought to manifest in justice displayed for others. Reading this chapter should cause one to again question many in the evangelical community who claim to know God yet socially deny justice to their neighbors. Most importantly, reading this chapter should cause one to look at themselves and evaluate the extent to which justice is evident in not only their actions, but their heart.

I was attending a pre-Thanksgiving dinner on November 26, 2014, with a group of my close friends. Full disclosure, most of those at the gathering were preachers, but on that evening, we were just the guys having a good time. Somehow the conversation shifted to the Ferguson, Missouri grand jury decision regarding the death of Michael Brown and involving Darren Wilson, the officer who shot Brown. As expected, everyone at the table was asked their opinion of the decision with virtually all agreeing that the decision was reached in error, but some unphased by the decision having been desensitized by other acts of injustice. Somehow as the conversation turned philosophical, one of my friends commented, "Humans are extremists!" He was attempting to make the broader point that human nature is to argue points at the extremes, but as I reflected on his comments I couldn't agree with that point. I interjected that I disagreed and stated my belief that humans are actually creatures of moderation. Almost six years later I still believe that we are creatures of moderation. The more I've reflected on my response, the more confident I've grown in its validity.

There is an anthropological argument to be made here, but there is also a biological one. Our very bodies reflect this pattern of moderation. Virtually every American student is exposed to the pH scale at some point in their K–12 science curriculum, and right in the middle of that scale is pure water—the substance that makes up roughly 60 percent of our bodies. Although it is slightly basic with a pH of 7.4, the blood that makes up roughly 7 percent of our body weight is also a generally neutral substance. While its pH ranges, our saliva, too, is a primarily neutral substance. Call me crazy, but I'm persuaded that the science of our bodies tells the story of what is optimal for us sociologically. Certainly, there are situations and circumstances where extremes are necessary. An easy example is the highly acidic fluid that fills our stomachs, without which there would be no digesting of food. Nevertheless, in the main, we thrive at neutral.

The application of the biological truth to our ideological positions is a theory that I have, rather predictably, called the *pH theory of justice*. Only in crisis do we go to extremes, and we do so only with the goal of getting us back to neutral. Acids break things down, and bases are used in cleaning. When acids and bases come together, we sometimes see violent reactions, not unlike the famous baking powder and vinegar experiment used for science project volcanoes.

That's where we are right now in America, we're at the point of one extreme and the other meeting face-to-face at historical flashpoints, and the result can only be conflict.

What I'm really describing is a viewpoint not too unlike what sociologists have termed *functionalism*, alternatively called *functional analysis*. As an undergraduate sociology minor, I spent some time dabbling in functionalism, which as a theoretical framework suggests that society has various parts and each part has a function that when performed helps keep society in a state of equilibrium.[2] I said "not too unlike" because the truth is we've probably never been in an ideal equilibrium. As far as functions go, consider that we could never exist as a society where every single person espoused a progressive ideology, or every single person espoused a conservative ideology. Society would fall apart if that was the case, if for no other reason than we would never achieve good policy. In some things you have to be progressive, like when it becomes evident that student loan debt is saddling a generation—the progressive thing to do is to provide some relief. In other things, you have to be conservative, like when it comes to amending the Constitution—you don't do that lightly; you do it only after intense consideration. There is a function for both the progressive and the conservative ideological viewpoints.

The pH theory of justice that I propose is to say that most of us really desire a certain level of balance, whether we can articulate it or not. Sure, there are the extremists; they have always existed in every society and always will, but the average Joe and the average Sue recognize the need for progression in some venues and a conservative approach in others. It really isn't until outside influences come into play that we begin to be skewed one way or another. Racism exemplifies this problem as it is clearly a learned behavior. People don't want to hate their neighbor, and the arguments they try to make about why it is okay to hate their neighbor almost always reveal an eventual hypoc-risy. It is exhausting trying to rationalize every action to support one's viewpoint. In the example of one of systemic racism's most blatant symptoms, police brutality, it has to be as exhausting for some police reformers to constantly suggest that every cop is bad as it is for some police leaders to deny the realities of racism in policing.

Throughout my decade and a half of adult life, I've watched the evolution of the race conversation. For what it's worth, when it comes to talking about race, our country is lightyears ahead of where it was fifteen years ago. The problem is that it is also lightyears away from where it needs to be. Analysis of even just the last two years shows how views have changed. A Civiqs daily tracking poll of registered voters showed that between 2017 and the middle of 2020 support for the Black Lives Matter movement increased in two weeks as much as it had in the two years before.[3] As of July 2020 51 percent of registered voters indicated support for the Black Lives Matter movement. The data reveals that the tide in public opinion about Black Lives Matter began to turn after the infamous 2017 Unite the Right rally in Char-lottesville, Virginia. The catalyst for that neo-Nazi gathering was the removal of statues honoring Confederate military figures. I was teach-ing sixth-grade social studies at the time, and I remember wishing the school year had already begun. I would've loved to have engaged my students at that moment in some conversation about those Confeder-ate statues. However, as fate would have it, public support for Black Lives Matter continued to increase, and as the school year began, there were plenty of opportunities to engage in meaningful conversa-tion. Those conversations would've never happened when I was a sixth grader in the same exact school district. Sure I was a black teacher, which made me a little more passionate about the race discussion, but more than that, it was evidence to me that times were changing. By July 2020, I knew that with even more certainty.

Florissant Road.

Racism isn't new, but in the grand scheme of history, the universal ability to capture and share video is. One has to wonder whether video technology would've abated police brutality over the years or whether it would've just exposed the masses to more of it. Every time I've thought, "This is it," or, "This is the video that will bring about a change," the next video has gone viral to remind me of what I said when I watched the last one. There isn't a single black person in America who can speak for all black people in America. Neither TD Jakes, nor Oprah, nor Barack Obama represents an entire race. But as a male member of that race, I can speak to the open wound that is re-salted every time I'm forced to watch a black man die at the hands of police on my Twitter feed. Even the completion of this book has been altered by the video of George Floyd, who died with the knee of a Minneapolis police officer on his neck.

People took to the streets to protest in Minneapolis just like they did in New York City in July 2014 after Eric Garner was killed, and just like they did in Baltimore in 2015 after the death of Freddie Gray, and in Baton Rouge in July 2016 after the death of Alton Sterling, and in Falcon Heights, Minnesota, in 2016 after the death of Philando Castile a day after Sterling. It was the protests after the death of Michael Brown that were a game-changer in the Obama presidency. These particular protests weren't the ones that occurred after officer Darren Wilson shot and killed Brown. These protests took place on Monday, November 24, 2014, after the grand jury in Ferguson decided not to indict Wilson. That evening, the world literally watched Ferguson's Florissant Road burn while President Obama spoke from the Brady Press Briefing Room just as cool, calm, and collected as could be.

If singing "Amazing Grace" the following year was a spiritual high moment for Barack Obama, failure to understand the emotion of that evening in November 2014 was the low point. For one, it was amazing to me that a president whose ascension was unmistakably boosted by great oratory could so completely miss the moment. Didn't he get it? On my television in front of me was the first black president stuck in a split screen with an event that was at its core a demonstration of the height of black anger. Florissant Road doesn't go across the country, and sure it was only a few streets in one part of a metropolitan area that burned that evening, but the anger in Ferguson represented anger across the country. The rocks thrown and parcels set on fire in Ferguson that evening were about more than the residents of Ferguson. They were about being sick and tired of being sick and tired of sons being killed with justice nowhere to be found. In that moment Obama, well into his second term, could've spoken to the emotion while still being measured in his language. The problem was that the split screen did him in, and the lasting image of that moment will be the president being cool while Ferguson was kindling.

And for the record, spare us the arguments about the deaths of black boys that occur at the hands of other black boys. Of course those lives matter also, and their deaths are wrong as well, but in those instances the murderers are hunted down and brought to justice. The problem is when the one doing the killing has a badge that enables him or her to take life. No badge should sanction extrajudicial killings. No police officer should be above the law. The only thing more upsetting than the continued unchecked killing of black individuals at the hands of law enforcement is the lack of understanding on the part of nonblack individuals when black individuals are angry about it. And then there is the chief ghost of rhetorical questions past: "If _____ were white, would the same thing have happened?" We all know that the answer is no. The Lord saw it, and it displeased him that there was no *justice*.[4]

Prophetic Lack

One of the beautiful things about the Bible is that throughout it one can find examples of central problems that reveal the heart of a nation at the time. Those central problems mirror contemporary issues. Throughout the text these examples reveal how the hearts of the people had strayed away from the God of the covenant, but their straying was not without a foregone calculus. The calculus (in error) seemed to be that there was some sort of benefit to be gained from putting their trust in something other than God. Wherever there is prophetic lack, there is also going to be a flawed calculus. One need only look at America's criminal justice problem, our lingering educational achievement gap, or gross wealth disparities and the pervasiveness of poverty to see glaring examples of prophetic lack. However, if present circumstances are any indication, we, and the powers we elect, are more prone to the numbness that characterizes prophetic lack than anything else. We are far too habitually desensitized to the cancers in our society, acutely aware of the symptoms, but consistently turning a blind eye to the causes of the suffering. Brueggemann presented a picture of the place that needed prophetic attention when he wrote, "Empires, in their militarism, expect numbness about the human cost of war. Corporate economies expect blindness to the cost in terms of poverty and exploitation. Governments and societies of domination go to great lengths to keep the numbers intact."[5] Brueggemann's identification of military, corporate, and government exploitation parallels sociologist C. Wright Mills's *The Power Elite* in which the leaders of those three sectors are identified as the most consequential trifecta of power in the nation.[6]

If one is to take a page out of the book of conflict theory, they would ask the question, "Who benefits from this arrangement?" Someone is always benefitting from the numbness. Why stop wars when the military-industrial complex stands to profit from government contracts? Why cease corporate greed when doing so would take some money from those who are so wealthy they would hardly miss it? Why advance legislation and policies that would bring about more justice when that would necessarily mean some sacrifices in terms of domination and imperial might? I've never considered myself a pure conflict theorist, but it's hard to argue with the notion that there is almost always a group benefitting from the arrangement. When there is prophetic lack the arrangement goes unchecked, and those who benefit can do so without any challenge.

Of course, there are always populations that endure a greater impact from exploitation than others. Historically the labor, the dollars, and even the insight of black people have been exploited. But just as we find in the Exodus story, exploitation has an expiration date. In 1994, in *The Prophethood of Black Believers,* J. Deotis Roberts prophetically declared that the United States was awakening to the reality of its growing multicultural population. Roberts wrote, "Nonwhite minorities are going to be powerful politically if not economically. As they become empowered, they will no longer be ignored . . . This pluralistic situation is the context for our decision and action."[7] Roberts gave us one of the key assignments of today's prophets—empowerment. Speaking truth to power is insufficient if such truth does not empower others, and sometimes it's just the prophet's language of newness that empowers people. The language of newness by itself might not represent policy change, but it is a potent weapon in any effort to change policy. Such language can be the catalyst for hope and the bedrock of the rallying cries that fuel movements. New language cancels out exploitation. It looks like the sermons that alert slaves to the fact that they are not property as their life on the planation might suggest. It's the exposing to the world of a dream that children might actually one day live in a nation where they're no longer "judged by the color of their skin but by the content of their character."[8] That's the language of newness.

Choosing Barabbas: The Criminal Justice Problem

No book could completely tell the story of nonprophetic America. No library could hold the volumes that would be required to tell the stories of the millions of men, women, boys, and girls whose lives have been negatively impacted by the pervasiveness of racism. In the same vein, it would be impossible to, in these fleeting pages, present the fullness of the criminal justice problem, as it goes beyond the police-involved shootings into deep systemic policy issues. It's in the stories that we find the personal impact of racism in criminal justice and policing. One errs if they focus only on mass incarceration; they must tackle the covert and overt racism in law enforcement and even biased laws that are used to lock individuals of color up in the first place. When black people reflect on justice and injustice, there are almost always personal anecdotes that come to mind highlighting the presence of one or the other. One such story took place on July 7, 2019, when Rodney Gillespie, his wife Angela, and their seventeen-year-old daughter were in a rental vehicle returning from a visit with friends in New Jersey. They were en route to their beautiful mansion in Chadds Ford, Pennsylvania, despite being in the US only temporarily. Rodney and his family were still living in South Africa, where he was overseeing the operations of a major corporation. They were back in Pennsylvania making preparations for a return to the States in a few months, right after their daughter finished high school.

Rodney was driving, the ladies were sleep, and they were just a couple of miles from their residence when a Pennsylvania State police cruiser began to trail them. If you look at the police dashcam video of this incident, you can watch the state troopers follow the Gillespies for several minutes and eventually turn their lights on to indicate a stop. The reason given by the officers was that Rodney had breached the line in the center of the road. But when Rodney noticed the flashing blue-and-red lights, he was only several blocks away from his home, so he proceeded to pull into his own driveway knowing it to be a much safer stopping place than the dark, narrow road their house is on. As the video captures, Rodney was rushed out of his vehicle and hand-cuffed on his own property. The state troopers didn't believe he and his family could possibly live in such a nice neighborhood. After several minutes Rodney was unhandcuffed and allowed to enter his home freely, but that was only after being yelled at by police, proving to them that he was the owner of the home, and receiving a petty summary citation for breaching the center line in the road. The Gillespies were released. Rodney's moment of bondage was temporary. But we find that too many times that is not the way the story ends when black men and women are in the grips of law enforcement.

In a world in which so much is viewable today, it's easy to view the continued systemic discrimination in our criminal justice system as just a unique contemporary American problem. However, such a view is not supported by a story that is referenced in one way or another by all four canonical Gospel writers. In Mark's Gospel account in particular, we find another scene in which there is an alleged crime and possible punishment, but in this scene the one in bondage didn't get to go free. The judicial district was Jerusalem, and the mood in the air was one of palpable unrest. Just hours before, the carpenter turned miracle worker that we know as Jesus was apprehended by the religious leaders of the community. He's mocked and spat on, he's roughed up and lied on, he's convicted in the religious tribunal on false charges, and then he's brought before the political power—he's brought before the government. No, he hadn't stolen anything, except maybe attention that was misplaced to begin with. He didn't assault anyone, except maybe the demons he exorcised from boys and girls throughout the land. And, no, this man didn't choose his identity, nor did he choose the circumstances that delivered him into the hands of power. Yet there he was, on the cusp of condemnation, all because those with whom power has been entrenched were jealous of him.

Fast-forward two thousand years, and the setting isn't Jerusalem but Philadelphia. The setting is Chicago and Atlanta. These and other cities display images just like the Palestinian city in Mark's Gospel, scenes of brown individuals, African American individuals, condemned to the vicious grip of mass incarceration. Trapped by the snares of the War on Drugs. Lives altered by calls for "law and order." Just like the condemned man in the text, many of these modern men and women are where they are because of the unspoken wounds of jealousy. For even today we find that when jealous powers can't control us, they'll condemn us. When jealous powers can't contain our message, they'll cause us to be maligned. In the example of the man in the text, the modern black man and the modern black woman find a clear contemporary. They find one who beat the odds and managed to make something of himself despite marginalization in society. They find one who doesn't come into the world born with a silver spoon in his mouth, yet nevertheless obtains influence and demonstrates that he can motivate people in a positive way. Naturally, this success engenders jealousy. This potential is a threat to those who only want to sustain power.

Like the ancient brown man Mark has presented, too many brown men and women today unjustly crowd not only prisons in my home state of Pennsylvania, but prisons across America. Here in the Keystone State black people are only 10 percent of the population, yet they're 47 percent of its prison inmates.[9] The American Civil Liberties Union (ACLU) of Pennsylvania says that the state has the highest incarceration rate in the northeast, and when the data is expanded to those who are on probation or parole, Pennsylvania has the second-highest rate of incarceration in the nation.[10] Prison operations are part of the economy and for many, help them maintain their power. In her groundbreaking book *The New Jim Crow*, Michelle Alexander notes that incarcerated individuals add to the census populations of very white and very rural areas, all while being denied the right to vote while they are behind bars.[11] Pennsylvania is no exception to this rule, as even within my own county, Chester County, the county prison has long been located in a sparsely-populated rural municipality. These additional bodies without voices in rural areas help keep power in the hands of some and deny power for others.

The biblical setting was all the more significant because it wasn't just any time in Jerusalem, but according to the text, the city of Jerusalem was at the religious, cultural, and civic height of the year. It was the season of Passover, and the annual festival caused the city population to swell. This was the yearly event that brought people into the region from places near and far. As such, the city was bustling with energy and was full of activity connected with this religious event. Yet on the civic side of affairs, the custom was that each year the political leadership would release a prisoner. Since it happened every year it was clearly tied to the social and economic cycles in the nation—it was expected. The Roman governor released a prisoner, and a little bit of favor was incurred to help keep rebellion at bay. Release a prisoner, and the chance of discontent was just a little bit lower. The political cynic might read this tradition as release a prisoner, and perchance the marginalized Jews could overlook some of the oppression they dealt with under Roman occupation.

The man who had been apprehended by the religious leaders was taken before the political leadership, and the political leadership—Pontius Pilate—just couldn't seem to find anything wrong with him. The Roman governor of Judea had examined this man looking for fault and looking for failure, but even with his thorough examination he could find no flaws. This left Pilate dealing with his own personal struggle. On the one hand he knew the man was innocent, but on the other hand political expediency meant he needed to satisfy the crowd, and the crowd would only be satisfied if the man was made to suffer. It is still the case that we find crowds getting their satisfaction from others' suffering. There are crowds outwardly satisfied when families are broken apart and children grow up without fathers. As disturbing as it is, there are crowds satisfied when sworn judges can accept kickbacks for sending young men to for-profit prisons.[12]

Although the setting of this ancient cinematic feature was the Passover festival, most of the extras in the production would've been unaware that the events taking place were much bigger than them. The scene there would've been one of the greatest wrongful sentencings in criminal justice history. There stood two condemned men, one deservingly, the other undeservingly. There stood two supposed criminals on center stage, one there by nature of his actions, and the other, according to the text, there by nature of his divinity. The man who deserved punishment was Barabbas, literally translated "son of a father." Barabbas, this son of a nameless and maybe even absent father, is an insurrectionist, a freedom fighter. He wants his liberties and freedoms. He wants to openly carry his guns so that he can fight against the government if need be. In fact, this son of *a father* wears a red hat that shows he wants to make his nation "Great Again" and believes the government is too involved in his life anyway. Surely the religious leaders had way too much to lose being associated with this son of *a father*.

They could've agreed for him to be released, but what good would an antigovernment man be to those who needed the favor of the Roman government to maintain their power?

According to the text, Pilate asked if it would be guilty Barabbas released or innocent Jesus. The crowd chose Barabbas. The American criminal justice system has a way of exonerating those it wants to exonerate and condemning those it wants to condemn. Again, we're led to ask the conflict theorists' question, who is benefitting?

Arguably one of the most powerful pieces of writing in the black theology canon is Howard Thurman's *Jesus and the Disinherited*. Although it only contains 32,000 words, each page is prophetic. In *Disinherited* Thurman wrote:

> The striking similarity between the social position of Jesus in Palestine and that of the vast majority of American Negroes is obvious to anyone who tarries long over the facts. We are dealing here with conditions that produce essentially the same psychology. There is meant no further comparison. It is the similarity of a social climate at the point of a denial of full citizenship which creates the problem for creative survival. For the most part, Negroes assume that there are no basic citizenship rights, no fundamental protection, guaranteed to them by the state, because their status as citizens has never been clearly defined. There has been for them little protection from the dominant controllers of society and even less protection from the unrestrained elements within their own group.[13]

Way back in 1976, Thurman understood that the oft-forgotten social standing of the historical human Jesus was too similar to that of the contemporary African American to be ignored. The marginalized Jesus of ancient Palestine mirrored the marginalized black individuals in Pittsburgh or any other American city. In one paragraph Thurman seemed to hit all of the important points in a way that it takes most scholars volumes to do: denial of full citizenship, lack of rights, lack of protection from the state (remember the government is supposed to protect), lack of definition of citizenship, the power of dominant individuals, unrestrained elements within the group. All of that, in one paragraph.

In the last decade few scholars have offered a more emotional critique of America's race problem than James Cone. His 2011 *The Cross and the Lynching Tree* is a powerful reminder of our present struggle with historical ills. Cone offered his own prophetic words on the criminal justice problem, "The lynching of black America is taking place in the criminal justice system where nearly one-third of black men between the ages of eighteen and twenty-eight are in prisons, jails, on parole, or waiting for their day in court."[14] Oh how little has changed from the moment that the ancient crowd chose Barabbas. Still today, at the behest of popular will, government will imprison black and brown individuals all while letting other criminal elements go free. Greed walks liberally while nonviolent drug offenders are locked up. Those who plot the demise of whole groups of people can do so with ease while young men and women who can't afford bail sit behind prison bars awaiting help.

Yet a prophetic viewpoint would be to believe that even in the midst of unjust political decisions, the same God that our money says "we trust" is working. Although it's uncomfortable and although it's not right, every unfair imprisonment adds another line to the story of a resilient people. Every tick up in the numbers of mass incarcerated black men and women contributes to what is already one of the most powerful narratives in history. That story tells of a people ripped from their homeland and subjugated into chattel slavery—yet they survived. The story says that there is a nation that like the one in Exodus

"multiplied the more they were afflicted."[15]

It should've been Barabbas condemned in that story, but it was Jesus. Pilate ordered Jesus flogged and handed him over to be crucified. If one believes the narrative, then a few things have to be accepted. If Jesus isn't crucified, he doesn't die. If Jesus doesn't die, he can't be resurrected. If Jesus isn't resurrected, death isn't conquered. Even injustice has a way of working out for the good. No, I'm not saying that injustice is right, quite the opposite. Nevertheless, it would appear that God has a way of vindicating those who have been wronged and making wrongs right. God has a way making good come out of evil, and catch this, sometimes it's just the writing of the story. Sometimes the good that comes out of evil is the story itself. Sure, the prison sentences remain, but so too does the potential for just individuals to bring about better. The potential is for you and me to democratically elect political leadership that won't disproportionately mass incarcerate particular groups of people and will reduce the sentences of those already in the system. The potential is for those who have unjustly spent too much time behind bars to do what Nelson Mandela did: be freed to lead the same people that bound him. Even as the crowd continues to choose Barabbas, the potential remains for a repeat of that one Sunday morning, when according to the Bible, he who was bound rose up in victory, renewed in body and spirit—rose up free. There is still potential.

ONE MORE SPEECH

A City Upon a Hill

As a final reflection in the language of the prophetic, we turn our attention to a phrase that originates from Jesus's Sermon on the Mount. The phrase "city upon a hill" was etched in American history when reverend John Winthrop invoked it in his 1630 sermon, "A Model of Christian Charity."[1] At the time, Winthrop was explaining to the Massachusetts Bay Colonists that their colony would be watched by the world, and that they should thus live and serve as examples to humanity. Today, the "city upon a hill" mantra remains a call for America to be a model nation, a call that I believe is completely valid and necessary, if not prophetic. Almost four hundred years later, the US has even more incentive to serve as that "city upon a hill" that Winthrop preached about. The founding principles that advanced our nation from the colonies of Winthrop's day to the federal republic of today were intended to make our nation a model for others, and in some ways have succeeded in doing so. Make no mistake, the world watches the US, and with the eyes of many other nations upon us, we do have a moral responsibility to provide the world with a positive example. Unfortunately, our moral leadership is now suffering.

The founding fathers were, for the most part, not overly religious men, but from time to time they referenced God. The Declaration of

Independence mentions God multiple times, most notably in the preamble when it describes, "the Laws of Nature and of Nature's God."[2] The other two primary founding documents shy away from religion. The Articles of Confederation avoid the topic, with the exception of government-authorized chaplains, some government subsidies for things like missions among the Native Americans, and the publication of religious texts. Likewise, the Constitution actually restricts religion's role, ensuring that there can be no "religious test" for public office.[3] That same Constitution was then amended by the Bill of Rights. The first clause of the first amendment ensured that there would be no national church, as was the practice in many nation-states, including England, the one most linked to our founding.

The language set forth by the founders in those documents reveals some key beliefs that have helped the US survive for almost 250 years. One of those principles involves restrictions on the relationship between government and religion. These restrictions were initially absent at much of the state level, but they were enacted from the start at the federal level. Such restrictions were intended to help the US avoid some of the dilemmas that were so prevalent in other nations. These were principles that came out of the Glorious Revolution of England, in which religious tolerance was promoted as the successful alternative to the strife between Catholics and Protestants. America's founders were less concerned with biblical truths than they were with just and efficient government. As such, theology was diminished, and at the same time the writings of philosophers like Locke, Rousseau, and Montesquieu were elevated. Natural rights, separation of power, and protection of property are but a few of the ideas that flow out of this time. The founders were all about that city that Winthrop had preached about; they just wanted it to be a city that had a foundation in something other than religion. Although our natural rights come from God, we are free in American society to choose our belief in the nature of that God. Similarly, powers are separated both in govern-ment and in religion. No religion will ever be embraced as a national religion. Religions even benefit from the principles of property rights embraced by our founders. We are generally free to seek to advance our own property, just like religions are free to seek to advance their own cause. The latter is singularly responsible for the significance of religion even today in the US.

If you asked me about American exceptionalism as an undergrad-uate student, I would've told you that the US should embrace a role as a "city on a hill." I would've told you that the eyes of the world are gazing upon the US and that for better or for worse, it is the most powerful nation in the world. That fact has been reinforced by a revi-sionist look at the Cold War. Over the years I've heard some suggest that in reality there was only one true superpower during the Cold War, the US. That status as the sole superpower remains unchanged from the days of Soviet-US tensions. Today the US has the highest GDP of any nation, and it's not even close. We even have the most powerful and technologically advanced military. When disasters like the 2010 earthquake in Haiti occur, the US is looked to first for aid and support. One of the most recognized humanitarian instruments in the world, UNICEF, was created in 1946, and since that time has only seen Americans serve as its head. That isn't a testament to the lack of leadership ability outside the US; it is a testament to the reality that American charitable efforts sustain UNICEF's operations.

Another phrase that Gospel writers attributed to Jesus states, "To who much is given, much is also required."[4] With or without the the-ology of Jesus attached, that phrase is commonly used as a positive lesson for all of humanity. It would be irresponsible for the US not to recognize its role in the world's eyes when conducting its own affairs. The challenge with being the city on the hill is making sure the hill isn't called hypocrisy. By way of example, it's easy for the US to pontificate about the illegitimacy of elections around the world, but when we allow our own elections to be stolen as was the case in 2000 with Bush v. Gore or 2016 with Russia, we diminish the power of our example.

The prophetic has a special relationship with the word *example*. A phrase from former president Bill Clinton's speech at the 2008 Democratic National Convention highlights the importance of the US's international example. "People the world over have always been more impressed by the power of our example than by the example of our power."[5] The world is watching us, but more important than the world watching us is what they see us do. With or without a high moral standard, and with or without noble intentions, the US would still be the leader among nations. Our economy and military alone command a certain level of respect. All the more reason why we should endeavor to be righteous (not religiously, but morally) in our actions. At that point in his speech, Clinton was talking about military restraint, specifically the use of force overseas. But I believe the chief way for us to be a city on a hill is for us to be consistent back at home. The ideals we espouse abroad should be validated by our work on the home front, especially in the way we treat our citizens. Justice cannot exist in a land of hypocrisy.

That three-legged stool of life, liberty, and the pursuit of happiness is great for middle school social studies classes. The phrase sounds good in speeches, and certainly paints the picture of a land of opportunity, but we should be concerned when so many members of our community are forced to live lives of struggle, are denied some liberties, and are hampered in their pursuit of happiness due to poverty.

The following is how the World Bank defines poverty:

> Poverty is pronounced deprivation in well-being and comprises many dimensions. It includes low incomes and the inability to acquire the basic goods and services necessary for survival with dignity. Poverty also encompasses low levels of health and education, poor access to clean water and sanitation, inadequate physical security, lack of voice, and insufficient capacity and opportunity to better one's life.[6]

If one needs an indicator that justice in a land has been turned back, they need only look for the presence of poverty. Poverty has always been a strong indication of injustice. If we use the World Bank definition as our framework, all of a sudden the last few years reveal the lack of justice, at least in the United States. There's the 2019–2020 coronavirus pandemic, which highlighted the impact of poverty on health, and the disparities in healthcare due to race. There's Flint, Michigan, which was ground zero for what can happen when those in poverty don't have clean drinking water. And of course pages could be written discussing the security challenges of impoverished neighborhoods. These are the consequences of denied justice. America didn't just get to 2020; it journeyed to 2020. It progressed and regressed to the present, rising and falling, growing and shrinking. Justice can't return without the prophets. There won't be any forward-facing justice if there are backward-facing *profits* masquerading as prophets. Will the prophets rise from the church as they have in the past? It's possible, but surely they won't rise from the church in its current form. In 2014 Jenson wrote something along those lines. saying, "The whole body . . . the socially recognized church, does not often fulfill a prophetic function in American society, and seldom has in any society."[7] If not from the church, then where? Quite frankly, I don't know. But it's worth it to circle back to president Barack Obama and consider him as one who could be a prophet.

Postpresidency Prophetics

I've already mentioned that sometimes people expect the prince to be a prophetic person. Such was the case with Barack Obama. Many people expected this big-eared senator from Chicago to be more than a president—they expected him to also be an American prophet. The problem is, as people would soon find out, prince and prophet are not only different roles, but they are also roles that cannot be fulfilled at the same time. There are plenty of examples of prophets displaying princely traits, like when Dr. King helped advance civil rights legislation during the Johnson administration. On the other side, there are plenty of examples of princes displaying prophetic traits. Abraham Lincoln is one such example. Lincoln's Gettysburg address, though only 272 words, concludes with the powerful language of newness. On the very same fields that not long before witnessed the blood and gore of the worst family conflict the nation had seen, Lincoln called for the birthing of something new. Not a new concept, but a new manifestation of that concept. The concept was freedom, and the presentation was prophetic. Lincoln said:

> It is rather for us to be here dedicated to the great task remaining before us—that from these honored dead we take increased devotion to that cause for which they here gave the last full measure of devotion—that we here highly resolve that these dead shall not have died in vain—that this nation, under God, shall have a new birth of freedom, and that government of the people, by the people, for the people, shall not perish from the earth.[8]

Nevertheless, Lincoln's prophetic presentation did not make him a prophet—he was still the prince. That nuance is important and holds true to this day. Since Lincoln's assassination at Ford's Theater on April 15, 1865, twenty-eight men have held the office of president. Although many of them have shown flashes of the prophetic, none of them have been prophets, not even Barack Obama. Obama has actually been noted for prophetic exceptionalism. Gorski and McMillan identified Obama's ability to "define America in terms of certain founding ideals—ideals of potentially universal significance which the nation tries but often fails to live up to" and recognized that he was "more reflective in tone and more apt to repent of America's excesses."[9] In that way Obama was very much like the Lincoln that he was known to admire.

Oratory has been at the center of President Obama's identity. In addition to the 2004 Democratic National Convention speech that launched him onto the national stage, there were a host of other speeches that helped make powerful oratory one of the lasting legacies of his presidency. One post-Obama analysis given just two days after his presidency ended cited his 2008 victory speech as his greatest one.[10] Other speeches that rank high include President Obama's 2016 farewell address, his speech after the Newtown, Connecticut, mass shooting, his speech commemorating the 50th anniversary of the marches from Selma to Montgomery, and his 2009 Cairo speech. Despite the obvious subjectivity that accompanies any ranking of speeches, the point remains that Obama's rhetoric and oratory will be one of the things people remember about him. However, the already described "More Perfect Union" speech is the one that best displays Obama's flashes of prophetic. No, he was not the president at the time, but as one who was well on his way to becoming the president, that speech is as much a part of his presidential legacy as any other.

In January 2015, as part of its "Obama History Project," *New York Magazine* questioned fifty-three historians on the probable legacy of Barack Obama. In her response to the question of **"What single action could Obama realistically do before the end of his term**

that would make the biggest positive difference to his historical legacy?" Annette Gordon-Reed of Harvard University responded with,

> I think he could do one more speech about race in the wake
> of Ferguson, Garner, et al. A speech that would reflect on
> the historic nature of his presidency and how it fits within
> the structure of problems we face today, and how we might
> go forward. I am sure such a speech would be ridiculed.
> There is so much bad faith out there. But if done the right
> way, it would help to shape his legacy. I do believe we will
> get better.[11]

Gordon-Reed's response to the question deserves some critical analysis. There were many interesting responses from the fifty-three historians who participated in the project; this one prompts an important conversation about the role of the Ferguson incident in Obama's legacy. The notion that "one more speech" about race could have helped shape Obama's legacy says a lot. For one, it speaks to the power of Obama's oratory, but it also suggests that there are others who recognize the missed opportunity that was Ferguson. That is not to disregard all that Obama did to advance race relations. Certainly, just by being elected and later by speaking to some of our nation's race challenges, Obama had a tremendous impact on our nation's understanding of race. But none of his words over the course of a first campaign and eight years in office solved the race issue, nor could they have. Now here in 2020 we find ourselves dealing with the ramifications of centuries of systemic racism. Sure, the nation grew more polarized during his tenure and our racial divide was more exposed, but ultimately if there was no exposing, we wouldn't have gotten to the place we are now in 2020 with systemic racism at the forefront of our national conversation.

The premise of the question was about Obama's historical legacy, not about history, and that's an important distinction. Again, we see the conflict between the princely and the prophetic. Even if at the end of his second term, President Obama had given the most eloquent and well thought out of speeches, it still would not have put him in the position of prophet. The prince delivering remarks that may or may not have been prophetic does not change that he is the prince. This is a good place to call back our friend King Saul. You may remember how Saul was told that his new appointment as king would be confirmed by his experience prophesying. Again, the text doesn't give us the language of Saul's prophetic expression, but we do know that he expressed it as the other prophets were led to ask, "What has come over the son of Kish? Is Saul also among the prophets?"[12] As it turns out, there are some striking similarities between Obama's "More Perfect Union" speech and Saul's prophetic expression. Neither Obama nor Saul was officially installed yet. One can make a case that as the clear frontrunner in the campaign Obama was well on his way to becoming the leader, just as Saul was the chosen leader having been anointed but not yet installed. In both instances, one destined to serve as a people's prince uttered to them prophetic expressions. Consider these words Obama delivered March 2008 in the context of the death of Breonna Taylor March 2020:

> The issues that have surfaced over the last few weeks reflect the complexities of race in this country that we've never really worked through—a part of our union that we have not yet made perfect. And if we walk away now, if we simply retreat into our respective corners, we will never be able to come together and solve challenges like health care or education or the need to find good jobs for every American.[13]

Barack Obama could've very easily been delivering those remarks in 2020, except he would've said the last few months instead of the last few weeks. Just as in 2008, there are complexities surrounding race that we haven't worked through. Just as in 2008, it is the case that to walk away from this moment in our history is to guarantee that this moment doesn't become a movement. To retreat from the conversation in which the oppressed name their grievances with explicit language like *white privilege, bias, systemic racism,* and *microaggressions* is to make certain that our nation will never come together to solve the many other social challenges, some of which have been explained above. That Obama's words can be read over twelve years later with the same application speaks to their prophetic power. On that day in 2008, one might've asked, "Is Barack among the prophets?" The answer to the question would've been the same as the answer to the one the prophets asked about Saul: no. Prophetic, yes. Prophet, no.

Things can change, though, and they do. Circumstances are vastly different when the once prince is no longer in office. It's not 2016 anymore, and Barack Obama is no longer beholden to public opinion, nor is he kept in check by the prospects of electoral victory or electoral defeat. The concept of a postpresidency prophet is one that has intrigued me for the last few years. But if anyone is in a position to do it, it is Barack Obama. I would submit that he has the capacity to be remembered more for prophetic work postpresidency than all of the good he did during his presidency. Such a transition would cement the legacy of a man whose tenure as prince was transformative in so many ways. And quite frankly, I'm not sure there is anyone in the world more qualified to be a prophet to the nation than one who has served the nation as its prince and transitioned out of that office honorably.

The question is then left for us, what does a prophetic postpresidency look and sound like? I believe that a prophetic postpresidency, at least in the model of Brueggemann prophecy, would look like a President Obama who breaks the mold of the traditional former president.

Tradition has held for much of our country's history that former presidents refrain from criticism of their successors. Such a practice can help avoid the weakening of the office and can help the former leader's standing as a father or (hopefully in the near future) mother figure. To truly be prophetic, President Obama will have to more frequently do what he has on occasion done, and that is speak forcefully to the challenges presented by the current prince. Most recently, President Obama's 2020 speech to the graduates of historically black colleges and universities spoke to the challenges of 2020 and the realities laid bare by those challenges. Obama stated:

> A disease like this [COVID-19] just spotlights the underlying inequalities and extra burdens that black communities have historically had to deal with in this country. We see it in the disproportionate impact of COVID-19 on our communities, just as we see it when a black man goes for a jog, and some folks feel like they can stop and question and shoot him if he doesn't submit to their questioning. Injustice like this isn't new. What is new is that so much of your generation has woken up to the fact that the status quo needs fixing.[14]

That's what prophetic language sounds like. It's the language of calling out the old and awakening the possibility of the new. As simple as it may sound, sometimes we just need a voice that's willing to put newness in the atmosphere. Sometimes we just need someone who is not afraid to say that the status quo doesn't work anymore. We might know that in our heart of hearts, but it hits differently when we hear it coming from a prophetic voice. Most of the attention Obama received from that address came from the fact that he broke with presidential tradition and criticized the current administration. All things considered the sentence or two in which Obama did that were pretty benign compared to what he could've said and how he could've said it. No one ever said that prophets can't use tact, but certainly they must be true to their mandate.

This particular graduation speech wasn't the first time Obama stepped out of postpresidency tradition. He also made waves on August 5, 2019, when he criticized President Trump's leadership in the wake of mass shootings in both Texas and Ohio. In a tweet that was mostly focused on the ridiculousness of continued mass shootings in the United States, Obama reminded Americans that "the El Paso shooting follows a dangerous trend: troubled individuals who embrace racist ideologies and see themselves obligated to act violently to preserve white supremacy." The more stinging language came when he addressed the Trump issue, writing:

> We should soundly reject language coming out of the mouths of any of our leaders that feeds a climate of fear and hatred or normalizes racist sentiments; leaders who demonize those who don't look like us, or suggest that other people, including immigrants, threaten our way of life, or refer to other people as subhuman, or imply that America belongs to just one certain type of people. Such language isn't new—it's been at the root of most human tragedy throughout history, here in America and around the world. It is at the root of slavery and Jim Crow, the Holocaust, the genocide in Rwanda and ethnic cleansing in the Balkans.[15]

But my favorite Obama rebuke of President Trump is the one that came September 7, 2018, when President Obama accepted the Paul H. Douglas Award for Ethics in Government at the University of Illinois. In the speech Obama named Donald Trump twice, in the first instance saying, "It [maintenance of the status quo] did not start with Donald Trump. He is a symptom, not the cause. He's just capitalizing on resentments that politicians have been fanning for years, a fear and anger that's rooted in our past, but also born out of the enormous upheavals that have taken place in your brief lifetimes."[16] Obama was speaking prophetically to not only the one in the White House, but also the possibility of a better future—a more perfect union. Notice the intentional use of the words *fear* and *anger*. Fear is always evil, but anger can be evil if misused. The apostle Paul referred to as much when he wrote to the church at Ephesus telling them to "be angry but do not sin."[17] The task for the Ephesians, and by extension us, was to recognize that anger is not only a natural emotion, but it is also a necessary one. If anger is to serve a purpose, its purpose should be to move us to the opposite of sin: justice.

All of us should be angry when we see the effects of racism. All of us should be angry when injustice diminishes the quality of life for individuals simply because of the pigmentation of their skin. All of us should be angry when the prince we have elected is found derelict in their duty. The challenge is not only to avoid sin, but to do justice. A related rhetorical question is presented in the 6th chapter of the book of Micah. "He has told you, O mortal, what is good; and what does the Lord require of you but to *do justice*, and to love kindness, and to walk humbly with your God?"[18] The calling is not only to *be* just, but to *do* what is just. That's why the language of self-righteousness that has typified the Trump administration should concern us. Not only is it lacking in humility, but it fails to call people to the *doing* part of justice. Not to mention that it isn't even just. Prophetic leaders present language that calls the nation to do justice. They recognize that ultimately justice has to be reflected in our actions. Kindness can't help but be evident when justice is being done. The people can't help but walk humbly when they're actually doing justice. Entreating our neighbor regardless of their socioeconomic status or race or creed or sexuality has a way of humbling us. Sacrificing some of our excess so that others can have their needs met has a way of humbling us.

Back in 2018 Obama pointed out that those fears and angers were rooted in the past. The last A in MAGA stands for "Again." The suggestion is that there is something to return to, and thus we should be angry about our current position. We need prophets who can counter that narrative. We need prophets who are willing to do the justice of speaking out in the present, not from the past but from the future. You're probably wondering how one can speak from the future? One speaks from the future by recognizing what can be. The future perspective is one of the hallmarks of the prophets. Prophetic people have to eat, sleep, and drink water just like everyone else, but what separates a prophetic person is their perspective. When you're a Martin Luther King and you're a prophet, you can stand at Mason Temple in Memphis, Tennessee, on the night before your assassination and say, "I just want to do God's will. And He's allowed me to go up to the mountain. And I've looked over. And I've seen the Promised Land. I may not get there with you. But I want you to know tonight, that we, as a people, will get to the promised land!"[18] With normal eyes King would've just seen another boycott and protest. With normal eyes, King would've become distracted by the crowds responding to his eloquence with claps and amens. But because King had a different perspective, his last prophetic public words were, "Mine eyes have seen the glory of the coming of the Lord!"

Barack Obama is not Martin Luther King. King was not and could not have been president of the United States. But in some ways Barack Obama is more positioned to be a prophet than King was. I don't know if that is what history will write about Obama when it's all said and done, but it sure is possible, and we've sure seen flashes of the possibility. Our immediate former president will surely give more than "one more" speech, and each speech he gives will be an opportunity to speak from the future. How awesome would it have been if the hill of Winthrop's righteous city was the same mountain that King saw?

The "hill" for a white cleric like Winthrop certainly would've been a mountain for a black man in the '60s like King. What both ministers did, and what I hope Obama will join them in doing, was call the nation to something better. Is Barack among the prophets? We shall see.

THE CALLED

Let My People Go

The biblical examples of prophets are of leaders who received spectacular calls at times when their God-given skills and abilities were most needed. There is an intense and inalienable connection between the calling and the needs of the times. Consider Moses, who according to Exodus was tasked by God with returning to the land he was exiled from to lead his people to freedom. Moses's entire story made him the perfect candidate for that particular prophetic assignment. Moses may have been a Hebrew, but he was raised as a prince. Moses had the blood of a Hebrew, but he understood the language of the royal household. Moses also had an innate sense of justice, which is what got him banished in the first place. (He killed someone in defense of one of his fellow Israelites.)

As America inches closer to more fully confronting its lifelong problem with systemic racism, it's worth it to consider the parallels to the Exodus story that has given us the name Moses. About 401 years ago, in August 1619, about nineteen black bodies walked off a Portuguese slave ship. Those individuals became the first African slaves in the British North American colonies. No, slavery was not new to the world, but chattel slavery such as that which was about to take root in North America was not the norm. Slavery had existed since the early days of human civilization, but when it had existed it usually served other purposes. Before slavery in America there were nations that had enslaved people as prisoners of war, nations that had enslaved people as payment for debts, and certainly nations that had enslaved people as punishment for crime. However, the United States, which didn't even officially exist yet, would come to be built on the backs of people who were enslaved just because of the color of their skin.

The story of blacks in America is a story that is so eerily similar to a people in north Africa that it's hard to ignore. That's one of the reasons why for so much of its history the black church has had a special connection with Exodus. The story tells of an Egyptian Pharaoh who along with his government set out to build the nation on the backs of slave labor. But the Bible is very clear that the more the oppression occurred, the more the oppressed people increased in number.

For centuries black men and women weren't even allowed to read the Exodus story for themselves, but somehow many of them could tell you the story. Oral tradition, of course, wasn't new, but undergirded by oral tradition, the story of the oppressed Israelites and their eventual release from Egypt was passed from enslaved black person to enslaved black person. Blacks saw an obvious link between the enslaved Israelites and themselves. They understood what it was like to be strangers in a foreign land and not wanted in a place that wasn't your home in the first place. The American slaves saw themselves in the story, but they also came to recognize the God of the story. They understood that the same God who brought the Israelites out would bring them out.

The American slaves had prophets just like Moses. There were Harriet Tubmans and Sojourner Truths and Nat Turners and others who rose up to speak as oracles of something greater than the present circumstance. The Exodus story tells us that when God got ready, he sent the prophet Moses to pharaoh to say, "Let my people go, so that they may celebrate a festival to me."[1] Just like those nineteen Africans who walked off the ship in Virginia, the Israelites went to Egypt as just a family of seventy persons. However, after four hundred years they had multiplied into a great nation, and the Egyptian powers understood how powerful those Egyptians had become. The Egyptians quickly became intimidated by the Israelites. We know Pharaoh was intimidated because he said it. He confessed that the Israelite population had become greater than the Egyptian population, and if there were not immediate harsh dealings, the Israelites were sure to increase and possibly even join Egypt's enemies in war. But the major turn in the story comes when pharaoh imposes new sanctions: Israelites would have to do the same slave work but with fewer resources—continue to manufacture bricks, but now without the necessary straw provided for them. In the process pharaoh lambasts the Israelites as lazy and says all manner of evil against them.

It's this part of the story, having to make more bricks while gathering their own straw, where I see the most connection to systemic racism in 2020. No, African Americans are no longer enslaved in a legal sense, but certainly black people are asked to make the same number of bricks but while gathering their own straw. Blacks as a population are asked to function in the same economy even though others are privileged in that economy. Some of the same individuals who are most privileged in the economy are the beneficiaries of generational wealth built on a cotton foundation that functioned on the backs of slave labor. Blacks are expected to survive in the same circumstances, with less support, and that, to me, sounds a whole lot like making the same bricks but gathering your own straw. According to the Exodus story, it was at the point of this particular oppression that God seems to indicate that enough is enough, and he sends Moses to pharaoh with a simple message: "Let my people go."

It has been a little over four hundred years. Of course, I'm not speaking of the Israelites in Egypt; I'm speaking of the blacks in America. Given all that has taken place in this season of America's story, one is led to think that maybe this is the moment for release. If you know anything about how the Exodus story ends, it ends with the Israelites finally being released and the system that oppressed them being decimated. Along the way there were some plagues, there were some false promises, there were even some disappointments and rejections, but the essence is that the oppressed were eventually released. They would not have been released, however, without the leadership and influence of a prophet.

Contemporary Prophetic Leaders

Above all else, prophets have always been called to extraordinary sacrifice. Among the low burdens of this sacrifice have been popularity and freedom; among the higher burdens have been peace of mind. Sacrifice remains a significant part of the call to the prophetic. On assessing twentieth-century theologian Reinhold Niebuhr as a prophet, Cone wrote, "Prophets take risks and speak out in righteous indignation against society's treatment of the poor, even risking their lives, as we see in the martyrdom of Jesus and Martin King."[2] Expounding on Cone's work and the prophethood of the black church, Croft wrote, "Cone compared King to the likes of reverend Henry Highland Garnet, Nat Turner, and the prophets of old."[3] Dr. Croft understood that there is a reason so many of America's prophets have come from the black church. Harold Carter called the African-American church the "connecting rod between African-American history and African-American hope."[4] Carter went on to suggest that the African-American church was the one place where "regularly the vision of nobler life is lifted up" and as a result of its independence from the dominant culture, "it is free to be prophetic."[5]

According to C. Eric Lincoln and Lawrence Mamiya, black churches vacillate between priestly and prophetic functions, with priestly functions concerning spiritual life, and prophetic functions concerning the political, with prophetic churches being "networks of liberation."[6] There is no doubt that the black church can produce Nat Turners and Martin Luther Kings, but to help reinforce the idea that the church is not the only place for prophetic leadership, I'd like to call attention to some of the prophets who are not clergy.

Today, academia is giving rise to a new generation of prophetic leaders. In the wake of the death of George Floyd, names like Michelle Alexander, Robin DiAngelo, and Ibram Kendi have garnered widespread attention. The writings of these and other scholars have helped give language to those working to end systemic racism and opened the eyes of those who aren't necessarily inclined to join the fight, but who recognize their own need for more information. The best evidence of this is the *New York Times* Best Sellers list, which chronicled the influence of these scholars. By June 14, 2020, after days of civil unrest, five of the top fifteen nonfiction books were directly related to race and privilege, including Alexander's *The New Jim Crow* and Kendi's *How to Be an Antiracist*.[7] By the following week twelve of the top fifteen nonfiction books were directly related to the same subject, including DiAngelo's *White Fragility* in the number one spot and Kendi's *Stamped from the Beginning* joining his other book. These scholars have dared to probe the history of America's original sin and describe it in language that the average person can understand. Their work has helped to inform a generation, and I'm persuaded that Alexander's book, in particular, will rank up there with the works of Frederick Douglass, DuBois, and others as essential reading in critical pedagogy.

I'll concede, though that academia, like the church, is an area that is easy to identify prophetic acts and prophetic people. After all, academics are paid to give lectures, instruct, and write things down. Since such work is etched into their job descriptions, there is a constant record of their thoughts and beliefs. Sports and entertainment are a little different. We generally expect our musical performers to make music, our athletes to win games or medals, and our actors and actresses to make good plays and movies, but among these groups we can also find some prophetic leaders. Take John Legend, one of my favorite singer–songwriters. One of the best examples of Legend's prophetic witness is the song "Glory," which he, Common, and hip-hop artist Rhymefest cowrote for the film *Selma*. Glory may be the most prophetic song produced thus far in the twenty-first century. In the opening line Legend rasps out, "One day when the glory comes it will be ours, it will be ours." The message of a better day is the epitome of the language of newness.

If one is to speak of contemporary prophetic acts, certainly they must call out the name Colin Kaepernick. Years before Derek Chauvin would put his knee to George Floyd's neck, Kaepernick took a knee to NFL fields, defying white supremacy, defying police brutality, and defying the president of the United States. As a result, Kaepernick lost the ability to play in the NFL. He literally sacrificed his football career for the cause of justice. Kaepernick is exhibit A for the burden of sacrifice borne by a prophet.

However, I'm reminded of a lunch conversation with Dr. Croft, who happens to be a mentor of mine and several others. During lunch our conversation turned to prophets, and Dr. Croft reminded us that prophets are rarely recognized as such in their lifetime. As a society we rarely appreciate the prophetic gifts we have until circumstances or, God forbid, tragedy takes them away. Even to the extent that America appears to esteem Martin Luther King as the epitome of a hero, he was not regarded as such at the end of his life. It is well documented that Dr. King's popularity was on the decline even among his contemporaries in the black church. Nevertheless, today most agree that he was a prophet.

Will We Listen?

There is no doubt that there are individuals in the field doing prophetic work. A more exhaustive analysis would likely find other sectors and disciplines in which prophetic acts are happening. As is the case when we find princes doing prophetic things, not all of those performing prophetic acts are actually prophets. Rather than ask the question, "Are there prophets?" we should ask, "Are we prepared to listen when the prophets speak?" This book is not intended to answer the latter question. And if it was, I would not have an answer. What I do know and can attest to is that we will not advance without prophetic leadership. Someone or some people are going to have to have the future-focused perspective to offer the language of newness and call society to the place of doing justice. If not, we'll repeat cycles of oppression and there will be an entirely new generation of victims. We err if we think we are so holy that we can't become a Nazi Germany or any other version of an oppressed state. A few years ago, many of us would've laughed had you told us that we would look on TV and see our national leader conduct himself in the manner President Trump has conducted himself.

In the wake of a global pandemic, things are vastly different than when I began this book over five years ago. COVID-19 has exposed the leadership flaws of princes, forced priests to redefine worship, and left all of us desperately in need of prophets. One of America's most underappreciated prophets, Maya Angelou, was quoted as saying, "Do the best you can until you know better. Then when you know better, do better."[8] In 2020 doing better is calling out evil by name and making sure we out systemic racism when we see it. Doing better is pressuring elected officials and advocating for sound policies that may focus on lifting some, but by doing so should lift all of us. Doing better means speaking the names of those who have unjustly lost their lives to injustices like police brutality. That means not only men like Travon Martin, Ahmaud Arbery, and George Floyd, but also women like Sandra Bland and Breonna Taylor (whose murderers are still free as of publication). Lastly, doing better means voting. On Tuesday November 3, 2020, citizens of the "land of the free and home of the brave" will have the opportunity to exercise the democratic right that God has given us. Together, we can prayerfully go to the polls and speak truth to power. We may not all be prophets, but twice a year all of us have the opportunity to undertake a prophetic act. With our vote we make sure those who are elected will be instruments of justice, including the president we choose.

The challenge is before us—we must embrace the hope for and possibility of better. A better prince to lead us, a priesthood that better reflects the Gospel it purports to preach, and a better sensitivity to the prophetic voices that rise among us. I still believe we're up for the challenge.

Notes

Chapter 1: Choosing Saul

1. *Merriam-Webster*, s.v. "prince," accessed December 9, 2019, https://www.merriam-webster.com/dictionary/prince.

2. Rom. 8:34

3. Juliana M. Horowitz, Anna Brown, and Kiana Cox, "Race in America 2019," Pew Research Center's Social & Demographic Trends Project, last modified May 5, 2020, https://www.pewsocialtrends.org/2019/04/09/race-in-america-2019/.

4. Adam Weinstein, "'We Are the 99 Percent' Creators Revealed," *Mother Jones*, October 7, 2011, https://www.motherjones.com/politics/2011/10/we-are-the-99-percent-creators/.

5. MSNBC, "Bernie Sanders Attacks the One Percent | MSNBC," YouTube, August 24, 2015, accessed April 10, 2019, https://www.youtube.com/watch?v=CHC9UKvrP2M.

6. 1 Sam. 18:7

7. 1 Sam. 10:22

8. 1 Sam. 8:1-18

9. 1 Sam. 16:7

10. Robert W. Jenson, *Story and Promise: A Brief Theology of the Gospel About Jesus* (Eugene: Wipf and Stock Publishers, 2014), 73.

11. Thomas Hobbes, *Thomas Hobbes: Leviathan*, ed. Marshall Missner (New York: Pearson Longman, 2008), 86.

12. 1 Sam. 8:11-17

13. John Locke, *Second Treatise of Government*, ed. C. B. Macpherson (Indianapolis: Hackett Publishing, 1980), 9.

14. Hobbes, *Leviathan*, 151.

15. John Dalberg-Acton, *Historical Essays & Studies*, ed. John N. Figgis and Reginald V. Laurence (London: Macmillan, 1907), 504.

16. 1 Sam. 10:3-7

17. 1 Sam. 10:10-11

Chapter 2: The Previous Prince

1. Larry J. Sabato, ed., *Divided States of America: The Slash and Burn Politics of the 2004 Presidential Election* (Harlow: Longman Publishing Group, 2006), 231.

2. Bruce Ledewitz, *American Religious Democracy: Coming to Terms with the End of Secular Politics* (Santa Barbara: Greenwood Publishing Group, 2007), 6.

3. David E. Campbell, ed, *Matter of Faith: Religion in the 2004 Presidential Election* (Washington, DC: Brookings Institution Press, 2007), 2.

4. Robert E. Denton, ed., *The 2004 Presidential Campaign: A Communication Perspective* (Lanham: Rowman & Littlefield, 2005), 32-33.

5. Campbell, *Matter of Faith*, 3.

6. John C. Green, Mark J. Rozell, and Clyde Wilcox, eds., *The Values Campaign?: The Christian Right and the 2004 Elections* (Washington: Georgetown University Press, 2006), 66.

7. David B. Magleby, J Q. Monson, and Kelley D. Patterson. eds., *Dancing without Partners: How Candidates, Parties, and Interest Groups Interact in the Presidential Campaign* (Lanham, Md.: Rowan & Littlefield Publishers, 2007), 23.

8. John C. Green, *The Faith Factor: How Religion Influences American Elections* (Westport, CT: Praeger Publishers, 2007), 65.

9. Kevin J. McMahon, *Winning the White House, 2004: Region by Region, Vote by Vote* (New York: Palgrave Macmillan, 2005), 83.

10. Denton, 258.

11. James W. Ceaser and Andrew E. Busch, *Red Over Blue: The 2004 Elections and American Politics* (Lanham: Rowan & Littlefield Publishers, 2005), 137.

12. Campbell, *Matter of Faith*, 10.

13. Paul Kengor, *God and George W. Bush: A Spiritual Life* (New York: ReganBooks, 2004), 292-293.

14. Ibid., 302.

15. Ibid.

16. Denton, *The 2004 Presidential Campaign*, 265.

17. Ceaser and Busch, *Red Over Blue*, 130.

18. Denton, *The 2004 Presidential Campaign*, 265.

19. William J. Crotty, ed., *A Defining Moment: The Presidential Election of 2004* (Armonk, NY: M.E. Sharpe, 2005), 23.

20. Denton, *The 2004 Presidential Campaign*, 271.

21. Ibid., 269.

214

22. Campbell, *Matter of Faith*, 4.
23. Ibid., 264.
24. Green, *The Faith Factor*, 10-11.
25. Sabato, 234.
26. Campbell, *Matter of Faith*, 18.
27. Denton, *The 2004 Presidential Campaign*, 259.
28. Ibid., 154-155.
29. Campbell, *Matter of Faith*, 8.
30. Sabato, 233.
31. Kengor, *God and George W. Bush*, 302.
32. Denton, *The 2004 Presidential Campaign*, 265.
33. Kengor, *God and George W. Bush*, 306.
34. Green, *The Faith Factor*, 144.
35. Magelby, 102.
36. Rozell, Mark J., and Gleaves Whitney. eds. *Religion and the Bush Presidency* (New York: Palgrave Macmillan, 2007), 115-116.
37. Denton, *The 2004 Presidential Campaign*, 272.
38. Crotty, *A Defining Moment*, 24-25.
39. Denton, *The 2004 Presidential Campaign*, 256.
40. Ibid.
41. Ceaser, *Red Over Blue*, 140.
42. McMahon, *Winning the White House*, 196.
43. Crotty, *A Defining Moment*, 27.
44. Ibid.
45. Ibid., 143.
46. Green, Rozell, and Wilcox, *The Values Campaign?*, 87-88.
47. Ibid.
48. Green, *The Faith Factor*, 142.
49. Denton, *The 2004 Presidential Campaign*, 264.
50. Green, Rozell, and Wilcox, *The Values Campaign?*, 67.

Chapter 3: November 4, 2008

1. Bush, George W., "Remarks to New York Rescue Workers" (speech, New York, NY, September 9, 2001), Selected Speeches of

President George W. Bush. https://georgewbush-whitehouse.archives.gov/ infocus/bushrecord/documents/Selected_Speeches_George_W_ Bush.pdf.

2. Obama, Barack H., "Remarks to the Democratic National Convention" (speech, Boston, MA, July 27, 2004), *The New York Times*. https://www.nytimes.com/2004/07/27/politics/campaign/barack-obamas-remarks-to-the-democratic-national.html.

3. Ibid.

4. Ibid.

5. McCain, John, "Acceptance Speech" (speech, St. Paul, MN, September 4, 2008), *The New York Times*. https://www. nytimes.com/elections/2008/president/conventions/videos/ transcripts/20080904_MCCAIN_SPEECH.html.

6. Ibid.

7. RealClearPolitics, "Election 2008 – General Election: McCain Vs. Obama," RealClearPolitics - Live Opinion, News, Analysis, Video and Polls, accessed November 4, 2019, https://www. realclearpolitics.com/epolls/2008/president/us/general_election_ mccain_vs_obama-225.html.

8. Dan Martin, "Impassioned Words from Jay-Z in Support of Obama," *Guardian*, November 5, 2008, http://www.theguardian.com/music/2008/nov/05/jayz-falloutboy.

9. Ibid.

10. GettingtotheTruth2. "CNN Announces Obama as the Next President Elect (Obama Wins Virginia then the Election)." YouTube. November 5, 2008. Accessed November 20, 2019. https://www.youtube.com/watch?v=9dKAKll1bUE.

11. Kyle J. Boyer, "A new beginning for GW," *The GW Hatchet*, November 6, 2008, A5.

12. Elaine Quijano, Alina Cho, and Jason Carroll, "Obama Win Sparks
Celebrations outside White House," CNN.com – Breaking News, Latest News and Videos, last modified November 5, 2008, https://www.cnn.com/2008/POLITICS/11/05/us.reaction/.

13. Keeanga-Yamahtta Taylor, *From #BlackLivesMatter to Black Liberation* (Chicago: Haymarket Books, 2016), 140.

Chapter 4: Hope and Fear

1. Barack H. Obama, "First Inaugural Address" (speech, The Inauguration of Barack H. Obama, Washington, DC, January 20, 2009).

2. Ibid.

3. Franklin D. Roosevelt, "First Inaugural Address" (speech, The Inauguration of Franklin D. Roosevelt, Washington, DC, March 4, 1933).

4. C-SPAN, "Total Scores/Overall Rankings | C-SPAN Survey on Presidents 2017," C-SPAN.org | National Politics | History | Nonfiction Books, last modified 2017, https://www.c-span.org/pre sidentsurvey2017/?page=overall.

5. John Sides, Michael Tesler, and Lynn Vavreck, *Identity Crisis: The 2016 Presidential Campaign and the Battle for the Meaning of America* (Princeton: Princeton University Press, 2018), 5.

6. John Swaine, "Birther Row began with Hillary Clinton Supporters," *The Telegraph*, April 27, 2011, https://www.tele-graph. co.uk/news/worldnews/barackobama/8478044/Birther-rowbegan-with-Hillary-Clinton-supporters.html.

7. Ibid.

8. Michael Tesler, "Birtherism Was Why So Many Republicans Liked Trump in the First Place," *The Washington Post*, September 19, 2016, Monkey Cage, https://www.washing-tonpost.com/news/ monkey-cage/wp/2016/09/19/birtherism-was-why-so-manyrepublicans-liked-trump-in-the-first-place/.

9. Barack H. Obama, "The President's Speech" (speech, 2011 White House Correspondent's Dinner, Washington, DC, April 30, 2011).

10. Lisa M. Segarra, "Watch John McCain Strongly Defend Barack Obama During the 2008 Campaign," *Time*, July 20, 2017, accessed October 17, 2019, https://time.com/4866404/john-mccain-barack-obama-arab-cancer/.

11. Tesler, "Birtherism."

12. Kenneth D. Wald and Allison Calhoun-Brown, *Religion and Politics in the United States* (Lanham: Rowman & Littlefield, 2014), 54.

13. Heb. 11:1

Chapter 5: The Resolute Desk

1. Steven Furtick, *Crash the Chatterbox: Hearing God's Voice above All Others* (Colorado Springs: Multnomah Books, 2014), 175.

2. Kevin B. Smith and Christopher W. Larimer, *The Public Policy Theory Primer* (Westview Press: Boulder, 2009), 50.

3. Ibid., 51.

4. Michelle Alexander, *The New Jim Crow: Mass Incarceration in the Age of Colorblindness* (New York: The New Press, 2010), 84.

5. Michael E. Dyson, *The Black Presidency: Barack Obama and the Politics of Race in America* (Boston: Houghton Mifflin Harcourt, 2016), 14.

6. Ibid.

7. RealClearPolitics, "Election Other – President Obama Job Approval," RealClearPolitics – Live Opinion, News, Analysis, Video and Polls, last modified January 2017, https://www.realclearpolitics.com/epolls/other/president_obama_job_approval-1044.html.

8. Ron Elving, "Obama Finds Reset Button With 2 Years To Go: Is It Too Late?" NPR, last modified December 29, 2014, https://www.   npr.org/sections/itsallpolitics/2014/12/29/372443996/obamafinds-reset-button-with-2-years-to-go-is-it-too-late.

9. Justin W. Moyer, "Why Obama Struggled in Ferguson Split-Screen Moment," *The Washington Post*, October 25, 2014, Morning Mix, https://www.washingtonpost.com/news/morning-mix/wp/2014/11/25/obamas-ferguson-split-screen-moment/.

Chapter 6: Strange Fire

1. Ozro T. Jones, "Sermon at Mt. Airy Church of God in Christ" (sermon, Preaching with Power, Lutheran Theological Seminary at Philadelphia, March 1986).

2. Robert Jewett, *The Captain America Complex: The Dilemma of Zealous Nationalism* (Philadelphia: Westminster, 2003), 54-55.

3. Leviticus 10:1-7

4. H. D. M. Spence-Jones and Joseph S. Exell, eds., The Pulpit Commentary (Grand Rapids: Wm. B. Eerdmans, 1950), *The Book of Leviticus: Introduction*, iii.

5. Lev. 8:30

6. Exod. 28-29

7. Exod. 28:42

8. 1 Sam. 16:7

9. Lev. 9-10

10. John C. Laughlin, "The 'Strange Fire' of Nadab and Abihu," *Journal of Biblical Literature* 95, no. 4 (1976): 560, doi:10.2307/3265571.

11. Ibid.

12. John 4:24

13. David Chidester, *Salvation and Suicide: Jim Jones, the Peoples Temple, and Jonestown* (Bloomington: Indiana University Press, 2003), 8.

14. https://jonestown.sdsu.edu/wp-content/uploads/2013/10/the-opendoor.pdf.

15. James A. Curry and Lawrence G. Felice, "Notes on Church-State Affairs," *Journal of Church and State* 21, no. 2 (Spring 1979): 376, doi:10.1093/jcs/21.1.157.

16. Marshall Kilduff and Phil Tracy, "Inside Peoples Temple," *New West*, August 1, 1977, 30-38.

17. David Chidester, "Saving the Children by Killing Them: Redemptive Sacrifice in the Ideologies of Jim Jones and Ronald Reagan," *Religion and American Culture: A Journal of Interpretation* 1, no. 2 (Summer 1991): 179, doi:10.1525/rac.1991.1.2.03a00030.

Chapter 7: The Black Church

1. Peter J. Paris, *Black Religious Leaders: Conflict in Unity* (Louisville: Westminster/John Knox Press, 1991), 19.

2. Wendell J. Mapson, *The Ministry of Music in the Black Church* (Valley Forge: Judson Press, 1984), 56.

3. Otis Moss III, *Blue Note Preaching* (Louisville: John Knox, 2015), 40.

4. Jon Michael Spencer, *Sacred Symphony* (Westport: Greenwood Press, 1987), x.

5. Mapson, *Ministry of Music*, 12.

6. Spencer, *Sacred Symphony*, 2.

7. Ibid.

8. Albert J. Raboteau, *Slave Religion*, (New York: Ofxord University Press, 2004) 233.

9. Spencer, *Sacred Symphony*, 3.

10. Moss, *Blue Note Preaching*, 41.

11. Ibid., 41.

12. Mapson, *Ministry of Music*, 2.

13. Raboteau, *Slave Religion*, 233.

14. Cleophus J. Larue, *I Believe I'll Testify*, (Louisville: Westminster/John Knox Press, 2011), 84.

15. Rom. 10:14-15

16. Rom. 8:26

17. Larue, *I Believe I'll Testify*, 33.

18. Ibid.

19. Ibid.

20. Spencer, *Sacred Symphony*, xi.

21. Ibid., 33-34.

22. Ibid., xi.

23. Rom. 8:26

24. Moss, *Blue Note Preaching*, 16.

25. Melva Wilson Costen, *African American Christian Worship*, (Nashville: Abington Press, 2007), 92.

26. Mapson, *Ministry of Music*, 15.

27. Wayne E. Croft Sr., "Worship Beginnings with a Never Ending: Revisiting the History of African-American Worship" (lecture, Worship in the African-American Tradition, Lutheran Theological Seminary at Philadelphia, Philadelphia, PA, September 2016).

28. Frank A. Thomas, *Introduction to the Practice of African American Preaching* (Nashville: Abingdon Press, 2016), 111-112.

29. Frederick L. Ware, *African American Theology: An Introduction* (Louisville, KY: Westminster/John Knox Press, 2016), 163.

30. Cynthia B. Belt, "Rap Music as Prophetic Utterance," in *The Black Church and Hip-Hop Culture: Toward Bridging the Generational Divide* (Lanham: The Scarecrow Press, 2012), 49.

31. Ware, *African American Theology*, 163.

32. Emmett G. Price III, *The Black Church and Hip-Hop Culture: Toward Bridging the Generational Divide* (Lanham: Scarecrow Press, 2011), 17.

33. Joy K. Challenger, "Infused: Millennials and the Future of the Black Church," (DMin. thesis, Duke University, 2016), https://dukespace.lib.duke.edu/dspace/bitstream/handle/10161/12921/Challenger_divinity.duke_0066A_10052.pdf?sequence=1.

34. Dyson, *The Black Presidency*, 220.

35. Challenger, "Infused."

36. Ware, *African American Theology*, 162.

37. Ibid.

38. Thomas, *Introduction*, 113.

39. Challenger "Infused."

40. Ibid.

41. Ware, *African American Theology*, 163.

42. Ibram X Kendi, *Stamped from the Beginning: The Definitive History of Racist Ideas in America* (New York: Nation Books, 2017), 442. 13. Challenger "Infused."

44. Ibid.

45. Arrested Development, "Fishin 4 Religion," on *3 Years, 5 Months & 2 Days in the Life of . . .*, Chrysalis/EMI, 1992, Cassette.

46. Belt, "Rap Music as Prophetic," 49.

47. Tupak Shakur, "So Many Tears," by T. Shakur, G. Jacobs, R. Walker,
    E. Baker, S. Wonder, Interscope, 1995, CD.

48. Tupac Shakur, "Blasphemy," on *The Don Killuminati: The 7 Day Theory*, 1996, CD.

49. Ronald B. Neal, "Beyond Fundamentalism: Reconstructing African American Religion Thought," *Journal of Race, Ethnicity, and Religion* 1, no. 8 (July 2010): 21, http://www.raceandreligion.com/JRER/Volume_1_(2010)_files/Neal%201%2008.pdf.

50. Michael Eric Dyson, *The Black Presidency: Barack Obama and the Politics of Race in America* (2017), 225.

51. Jordan Fabian, "Trump Hosts Kanye for Surreal Oval Office Meeting," *The Hill*, October 11, 2018, accessed March 2, 2020, https://thehill.com/homenews/administration/410989-trump-meets-kanye-at-surreal-oval-office-meeting.

52. Kanye West, *Jesus Walks*, Sony, 2004, CD.

53. Kylee C. Smith, "Black Women's Bodies in American Culture and Performance," (master's thesis, Ohio State University, 2017), https:// kb.osu.edu/dspace/bitstream/handle/1811/80525/Kylee_Smith_ Thesis.pdf?sequence=1.

54. Chance the Rapper, "How Great," in *Coloring Book*, Self-released, 2016, Mixtape.

55. Chance the Rapper, *Coloring Book*, Self-released, 2016, Mixtape.

56. Chance the Rapper, "Blessings," in *Coloring Book*, Self-Released, 2016, Mixtape.

57. Barack H. Obama, "A More Perfect Union" (speech, delivered at the National Constitution Center, Philadelphia, PA, March 18, 2008).

58. Jeremiah A. Wright, "Confusing God and Government" (sermon, delivered at Trinity United Church of Christ, Chicago, IL, April 13, 2003).

59. BlackPast, "(2003) Rev. Jeremiah Wright, 'Confusing God and Government,'" BlackPast, last modified September 24, 2019, https:// www.blackpast.org/african-american-history/2008-rev-jeremiahwright-confusing-god-and-government/.

Chapter 8: Amazing Grace

1. Lynne A. DeSpelder and Albert L. Strickland, *The Path Ahead: Readings in Death and Dying* (Mountain View, CA: Mayfield Publishing, 1995), 80.

2. Jacqueline S. Thursby, *Funeral Festivals in America: Rituals for the Living* (Lexington: University Press of Kentucky, 2006), 38.

3. DeSpelder and Strickland, *The Path Ahead*, 92.

4. Karla F. C. Holloway, *Passed On: African American Mourning Stories, A Memorial* (Durham: Duke University Press, 2002), 21.

5. Thursby, *Funeral Festivals*, 22.

6. Pat Berman, "In Death Keeping Tradition Alive," *The State*, July 31, 2003, 2, https://poststar.com/lifestyles/in-death-keeping-traditionalive/article_a8ad7330-fc70-5fe5-9828-a95cf9f1ee27.html.

7. Cynthia A. Peveto and Bert Hayslip, Jr., *Cultural Changes in Attitudes Toward Death, Dying, and Bereavement* (New York: Springer Publishing Company, 2005), 31.

8. Thursby, *Funeral Festivals*, 52.

9. Peveto and Hayslip, Jr., *Cultural Changes*, 33.

10. Ibid, 37.

11. Thursby, *Funeral Festivals*, 99.

12. Holloway, *Passed On*, 25.

13. Peveto and Hayslip, Jr., *Cultural Changes*, 38.

14. Michael R. Leming and George E. Dickinson, *Understanding Dying, Death, & Bereavement* (Belmont, CA: Thomson/Wadsworth, 2007), 102.

15. Peveto and Hayslip, Jr., *Cultural Changes*, 35.

16. Ibid., 32.

17. Ibid., 33.
18. Leming and Dickinson, *Understanding Dying*, 102.
19. Holloway, *Passed On*, 150.
20. Ibid., 155.
21. Ibid., 150.
22. Holloway, *Passed On*, 178.
23. Washington Post Staff, "Transcript: Obama delivers eulogy for Charleston pastor, the Rev. Clementa Pinckney," *The Washington Post*, last modified June 26, 2015, https://www.washingtonpost.com/ news/post-nation/wp/2015/06/26/transcript-obama-deliverseulogy-for-charleston-pastor-the-rev-clementa-pinckney/.
24. Henry H. Mitchell, *Black Preaching: The Recovery of a Powerful Art* (Nashville: Abingdon Press, 1990), 115.
25. Washington Post Staff, "Transcript."
26. *Merriam-Webster*, s.v. "grace," accessed March 2, 2020, https://www.merriam-webster.com/dictionary/grace.
27. Mitchell, *Black Preaching*, 122.
28. Washington Post Staff, "Transcript."

Chapter 9: Two Priesthoods

1. 2 Kings 20:1-11; 2 Chron. 32:24-26; Isa. 38
2. Isa. 38:3
3. 2 Kings 18:3
4. 2 Kings 18:4
5. 2 Kings 20:1; Isa. 38:1
6. Neh. 1:5
7. Neh. 1:11
8. Ps. 66:18
9. James 5:16
10. Prov. 1:25-26
11. Isiah 38:3
12. Isa. 38:5
13. Louis H. Feldman, "Josephus's Portrait of Hezekiah," *Journal of Biblical Literature* 111, no. 4 (1992): 597-610, doi:10.2307/3267434.

14. Forrest Church, So Help Me God: The Founding Fathers and the First Great Battle Over Church and State (Boston: Houghton Mifflin Harcourt, 2008), 8.

15. 1 Tim. 2:2

16. Ps. 2:10-11

17. Associated Press, "Trump: Both Sides to Blame for Charlottesville," YouTube, August 20, 2017, https://www.youtube. com/watch?v=Q10kZKBm8Vc.

18. "Missional Vocation: Called and Sent to Represent the Reign of God," in *Missional Church: A Vision for the Sending of the Church in North America*, ed. Daniel L. Guder (Grand Rapids: Wm. B. Eerdmans Publishing, 1998), 109.

19. Betsy DeVos, "Interview with Betsy DeVos, the Reformer," by Philanthropy Roundtable, Philanthropy Today, last modified Spring 2013, https://www.philanthropyroundtable.org/ philanthropy-magazine/article/spring-2013-interview-with-betsydevos-the-reformer.

20. Betsy DeVos, "Prepared Remarks from U.S. Secretary of Education Betsy DeVos to Foundation for Excellence in Education

National Summit on Education Reform" (speech, Excellence in Education National Summit on Education Reform, Nashville, Tennessee, November 30, 2017).

21. The National Commission on Excellence in Education, *A Nation At Risk: The Imperative for Educational Reform*, (Washington, DC: The National Commission on Excellence in Education, 1983).

22. POLITICO, "Betsy and Dick DeVos Talk About Reforming Education at a Gathering of Wealthy Christians in 2001," POLITICO, last modified December 2, 2016, https://www.politico. com/video/2016/12/betsy-and-dick-devos-talk-about-reformingeducation-at-a-gathering-of-wealthy-christians-in-2001-061697.

Chapter 10: The Alternative

1. Walter Brueggemann, *The Prophetic Imagination*, (Philadelphia: Fortress Press, 1978), 13.

2. Jer. 2:16

3. Jer. 5:30-31

4. Hosea 3:1

5. Mic. 6:2

6. Mic. 7:9

7. A. H. Maslow, "A Theory of Human Motivation," *Psychological Review* 50, no. 4 (1943): xx, doi:10.1037/h0054346.

8. *Hitchcock's Dictionary of Bible Names*, s.v. "Sanballat," accessed February 2, 2019, https://www.biblestudytools.com/dictionaries/hitchcocks-bible-names/sanballat.html.

9. Brueggemann, *Prophetic Imagination*, 9.

10. Julie Hirschfeld Davis and Peter Baker, "How the Border Wall Is Boxing Trump In," *The New York Times*, January 5, 2019, https://www.nytimes.com/2019/01/05/us/politics/donald-trump-borderwall.html.

11. Langston Hughes, "Let America Be America Again," *Présence Africaine* 59, no. 3 (1966): 3-5, doi:10.3917/presa.059.0003.

12. Ibid., 23.

13. Katharine L. Bates, *America the Beautiful: And Other Poems* (New York: Thomas Y. Crowell Company, 1911), 3-4, https://archive.org/details/americabeautiful00batcrich/mode/2up.

14. Wald and Calhoun-Brown, *Religion and Politics*, 58.

Chapter 11: When Justice Is Turned Back

1. Isiah 59:4,9,14-15

2. James M. Henslin, "The Sociological Perspective," in *Sociology: A Down-To-Earth Approach* (Boston: Allyn & Bacon, 2007), 2-31.

3. Nate Cohn and Kevin Quealy, "How Public Opinion Has Moved on Black Lives Matter," The New York Times - Breaking News, World News & Multimedia, last modified June 10, 2020, https://www. nytimes.com/interactive/2020/06/10/upshot/black-lives-matterattitudes.html.

4. Isiah 59:15

5. Brueggemann, *Prophetic Imagination*, 85.

6. C. Wright Mills, The Power Elite (New York: Oxford University Press, 1956).

7. J. Deotis Roberts, *The Prophethood of Black Believers: An African American Political Theology for Ministry*, (Louisville: Westminster/ John Knox Press, 1994), 32.

8. Martin Luther King, Jr., "I Have a Dream" (speech, March on Washington, Washington, DC, August 28, 1963).

9. Prison Policy Initiative, "Pennsylvania Profile," Prison Policy Initiative, accessed March 12, 2020, https://www.prisonpolicy.org/profiles/PA.html.

10. ACLU Pennsylvania, "Smart Justice PA," ACLU Pennsylvania, last modified December 4, 2019, https://www.aclupa.org/en/campaigns/smart-justice-pa. 11. Alexander, *New Jim Crow*, 240.

12. Ian Urbina, "Despite Red Flags About Judges, a Kickback Scheme Flourished," *The New York Times*, March 27, 2009.

13. Howard Thurman, *Jesus and the Disinherited* (Boston: Beacon Press, 1976), 23-24.

14. James H. Cone, *The Cross and the Lynching Tree* (Maryknoll: Orbis Books, 2011), 163.

15. Exod. 1:12

Chapter 12: One More Speech

1. John Winthrop, "John Winthrop: A Modell of Christian Charity, 1630," History Department : Hanover College, last modified 1630, https://history.hanover.edu/texts/winthmod.html.

2. "Declaration of Independence: A Transcription," National Archives, last modified November 19, 2019, https://www.archives.gov/founding-docs/declaration-transcript. U.S. Constitution, art. 6, cl. 3

3. Luke 12:48

4. Bill Clinton, "Speech" (lecture, 2008 Democratic National Convention, Denver, Colorado, August 27, 2008).

5. Jonathan Haughton and Shahidur R. Kkandker, *Handbook on Poverty and Inequality* (Washington, DC: World Bank, 2009), 1-2.

6. Jenson, *Story and Promise*, 86.

7. Abraham Lincoln, "The Gettysburg Address" (speech, Gettysburg, Pennsylvania, November 19, 1863).

8. Philip S. Gorski and William McMillan, "Barack Obama and American Exceptionalisms," *The Review of Faith & International Affairs* 10, no. 2 (2012): 41-50, doi:10.1080/15570274.2012.682513.

9. Patterson, Thom. "Rating President Obama's Biggest Speeches." CNN. Last modified January 23, 2017. https://www.cnn.com/2017/01/18/politics/speeches-the-end-last-days-obamawhite-house/index.html.

10. 1 Sam. 10:11

11. Annette Gordon-Reed, "Obama History Project - Annette Gordon-Reed," NYMag.com, last modified January 11, 2015, https://nymag.com/news/politics/obama-history-project/annette-gordon-reed/.

12. Obama, "A More Perfect Union."

13. Rebecca Falconer, "Read: Obama Tells HBCU Graduates Pandemic Spotlights Underlying Burdens of Black Communities," Axios, last modified May 17, 2020, https://www.axios.com/read-obamadelivers-hbcu-commencement-speech-ab461eec-7ee4-42ff-ad52a7373afaa4f1.html.

14. Barack Obama, Twitter post, August 5, 2019, 3:01 p.m., https://twitter.com/BarackObama/status/1158453079035002881.

15. Libby Nelson, "Read the Full Transcript of Obama's Fiery Anti-Trump Speech," Vox, last modified September 7, 2018, https://www.vox.com/policy-and-politics/2018/9/7/17832024/obamaspeech-trump-illinois-transcript.

16. Eph. 4:26

17. Mic. 6:8

18. Martin Luther King, Jr., "Martin Luther King's Final Speech: 'I've Been to the Mountaintop' – The Full Text," ABC News, last modified April 3, 2013, https://abcnews.go.com/Politics/martin-lutherkings-final-speech-ive-mountaintop-full/story?id=18872817.

Chapter 13: The Called

1. Exod. 5:1

2. James H. Cone, *Cross and the Lynching Tree*, 61.

3. Wayne E. Croft Sr., *The Motif of Hope in African American Preaching During Slavery and the Post-Civil War Era: There's a Bright Side Somewhere* (Lanham: Lexington Books, 2017), 11.

4. Harold A. Carter, Wyatt Tee Walker and William A. Jones, Jr., *The African American Church: Past, Present, and Future* (New York: Martin Luther King, Jr., Fellows Press 1991), 96.

5. Ibid.

6. C. Eric Lincoln and Lawrence Mamiya, *The Black Church in the African American Experience* (Durham: Duke University Press, 1990), 11-16.

7. *The New York Times*, "Best Sellers – June 14, 2020 – *The New York Times*," *The New York Times* – Breaking News, World News & Multimedia, last modified June 14, 2020, https://www.nytimes.com/books/best-sellers/2020/06/14/.

8. Maya Angelou, "A Quote by Maya Angelou," Goodreads | Meet Your Next Favorite Book, accessed July 1, 2020, https://www.goodreads.com/quotes/7273813-do-the-best-you-can-until-youknow-better-then.